SUTURE SELF

A Book of Medical Cartoons

by *New Yorker* Cartoonist Leo Cullum

Andrews McMeel
Publishing, LLC

Kansas City

09 10 11 12 13 SDB 10 9 8 7 6 5 4 3 2 1

ISBN-13: 978-0-7407-8015-8
ISBN-10: 0-7407-8015-8

Library of Congress Control Number: 2008935762

www.andrewsmcmeel.com

ATTENTION: SCHOOLS AND BUSINESSES

This book is dedicated to good friends and good doctors:

Irv and Marcy Frankel; Joe Giacinto; Tom and Pat Gamble; Greg Hodal; Jim and Rosemary Bell; Phil Martorelli; Pete O'Connor; Doug Ryan; Frank Garvey; Mark Brown; Kay Lenz; Cliff and Cecelia Waeschle; Gayle and Sid Minnick; Sandy and Terry Ronan; Jonathan and Genny Banks; Leonard Skurro; Carrieann Carson; Christine and Dennis Rodgerson; Greg, Lynnrae, and all the McClintocks; Doug Seay; Art Tozzi; Bob Beavis; Hannah, Judith, and Van Schley; Lisa and Larry Waldinger; Caroline and Sidney Kimmel; Charles Tobias; Debi and Danny Boyle; Casey Sander; Dave Thomas; Edward Edwards; Rupert and Karen Hitzig; Carl Volante; David Hardie; Marcus Berry; Evan Nicholas; and Tom Cullum.

Dr. Barry Rosenbloom, Dr. Ed Phillips, Dr. Steven Colquhoun, Dr. Zev Wainberg, Dr. Ross Donehower, Dr. Lisa Benya, Dr. Tom Hirsch, Dr. James Sternberg, Mary Grace Brandon, Jose Ramirez, Sandy Labat, and all the staff at Tower Oncology.

Most especially to my wife, Kathy, and my daughters, Kimberly and Kaitlin.

Introduction

A book of doctor cartoons . . . Why now? Why doctors? Well, "now" because I needed the $500 advance, and "doctors" because lawyers will sue in a heartbeat. And who wants to be a heartbeat away from a lawsuit or from a lawyer?

Who are these people who want to probe other peoples' naked bodies? At my gym, I've seen several naked doctors but kept my hands to myself.

From whence arises the desire to be a doctor? From a boundless intellectual curiosity, a deep wellspring of goodwill, a small black bag of altruism, a longing for a Mercedes?

I have several friends who are doctors, and they seem normal enough or at least what passes for normal in Southern California. I know I'm their friend because I'm allowed to call them by their first names. I do maintain a certain amount of deference toward them and occasionally slip into subservience, but that is something I should take up with my psychiatrist.

They hardly seem to mind when, at lunch, I'll ask, "Would you mind taking a look at this?" I've actually gotten second opinions from waiters.

My mother wanted me to be a doctor. She really just wanted to say, "My son, the doctor," which she said anyway. Doctor . . . cartoonist . . . Why quibble?

Being a doctor might have been nice—walking around in pajamas . . . OK, scrubs . . . all day, accessing celebrities' health records, cruising on the yacht, secure in the knowledge that, despite the numerous advances in preventative health care, people would continue to get sick. Two roads diverged in a wood and I took the one less compensated.

But, I'm not complaining. OK, I'm complaining. I just never had any desire to be a doctor. I am glad, though, we have so many dedicated and capable people who want to take on this demanding career.

Lately I've been in touch with a lot of doctors and, in spite of some of the drawings in this collection, I salute all the practitioners and supporters of the medical arts. I have received excellent care. In fact, at my last appointment my doctor was able to report that I now have the bank account of a man half my age.

"I'm feeling a tightness in my wallet."

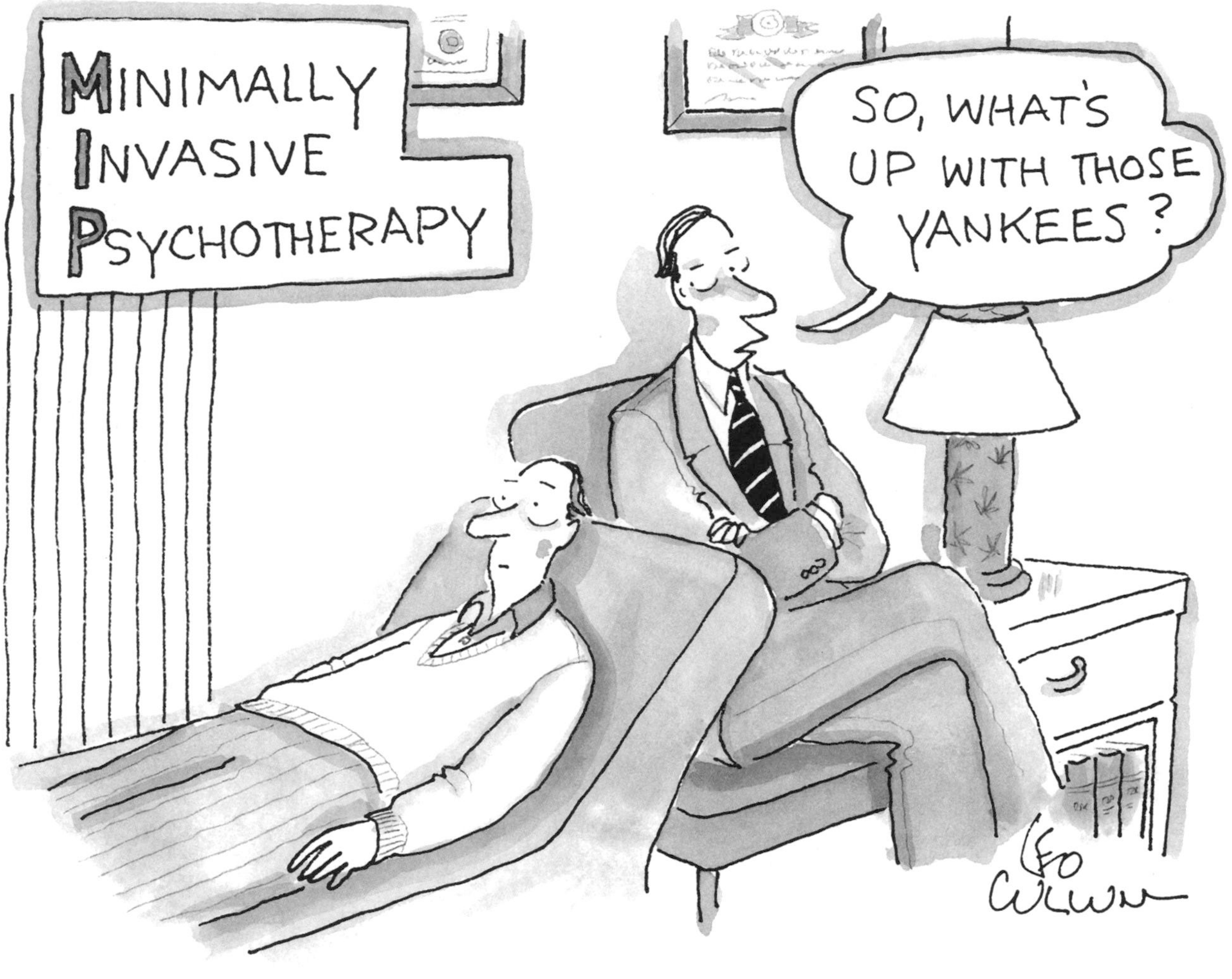
MINIMALLY
INVASIVE
PSYCHOTHERAPY
SO, WHAT'S UP WITH THOSE YANKEES ?

"It's an experimental medicine. We're trying some at fourteen dollars and some at forty-nine."

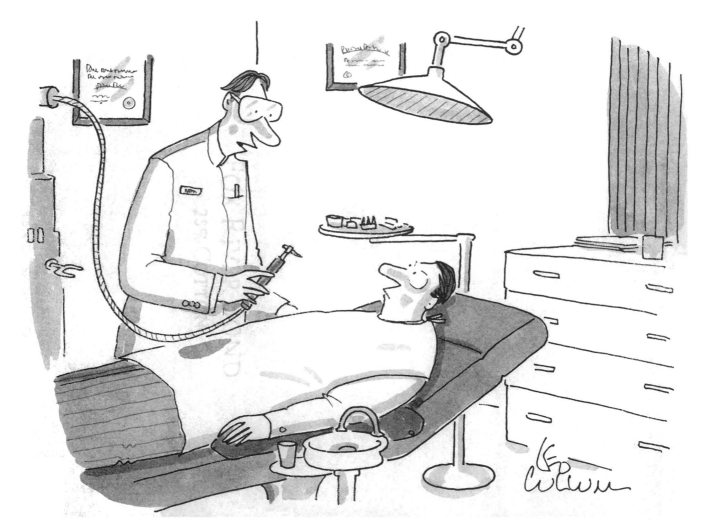

"If a root canal doesn't hurt, it isn't being done right."

"I'm taking my Viagra with Prozac. If it doesn't work I don't care."

"I found it! I mistakenly had you in the dead file."

"Water...Depth...Deep...Deep...Depressed?"

"Dr. Rosenbloom, from special operations, will do the surgery."

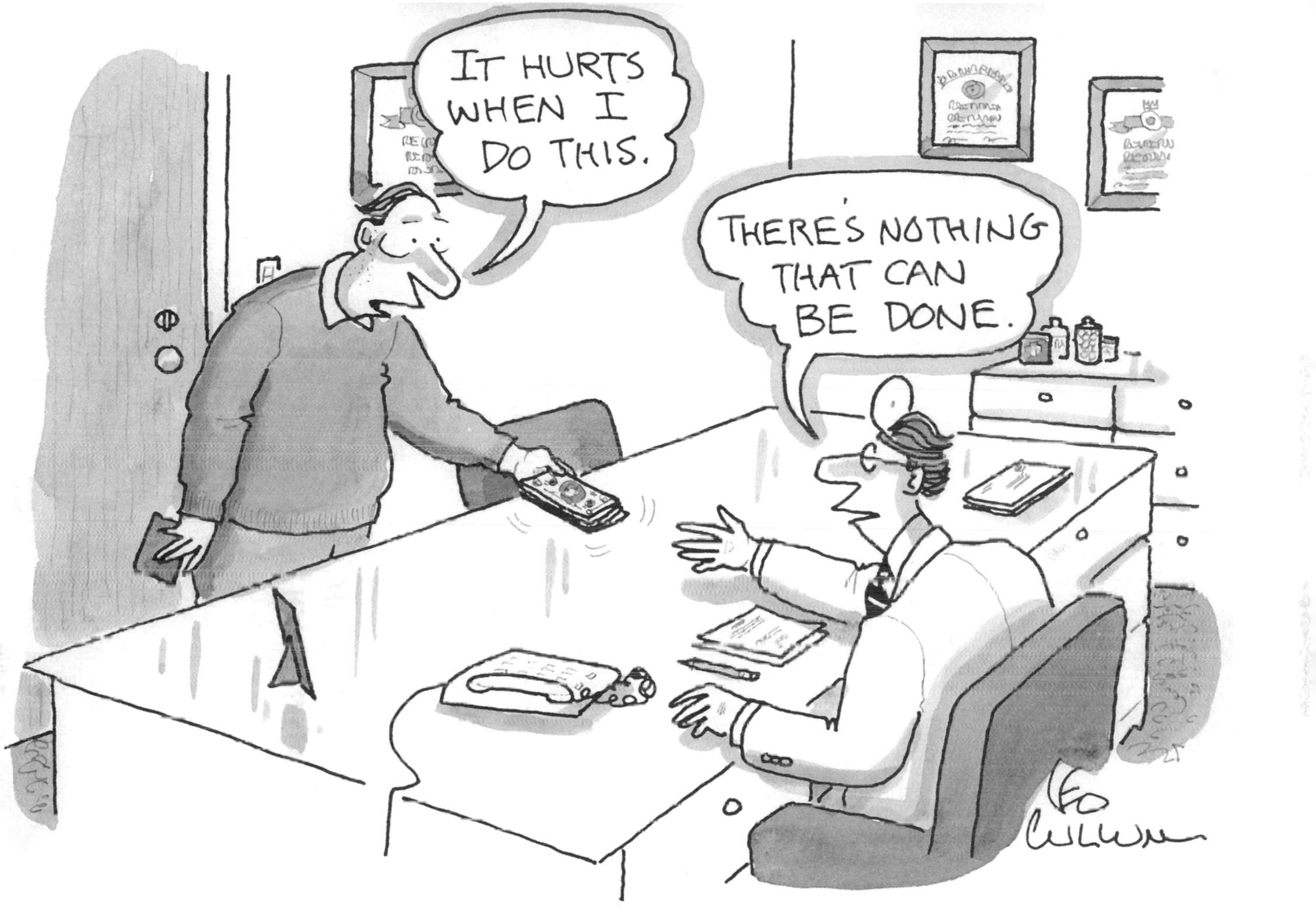
IT HURTS WHEN I DO THIS.
THERE'S NOTHING THAT CAN BE DONE.

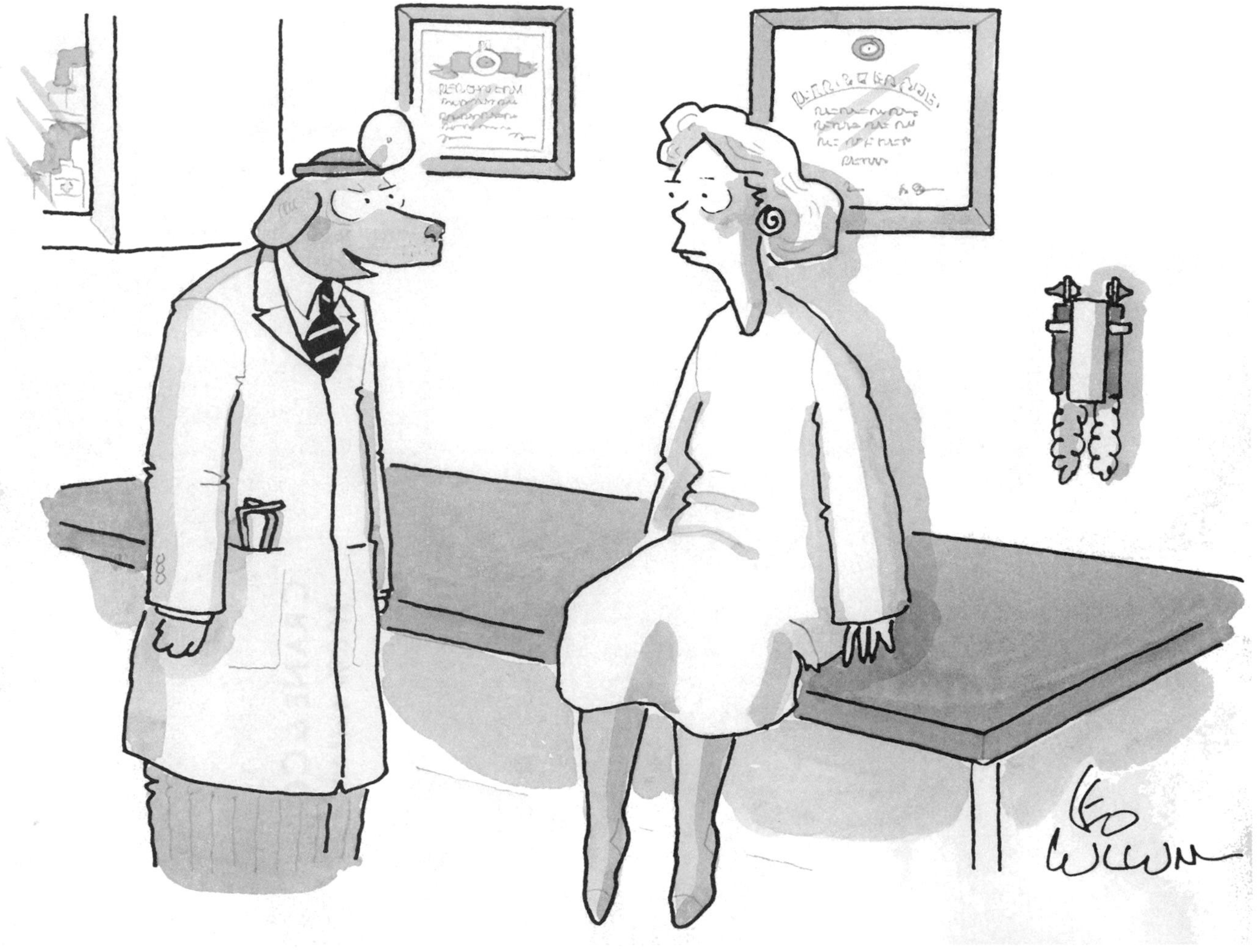

"Get rid of your cats."

"Turn his head to the right and cough."

"Of course I'm a real doctor. Would I be sticking you with this big needle if I were a clown?"

"Would you step to the side? They're still doing CPR."

"You have an 'achey breaky' heart."

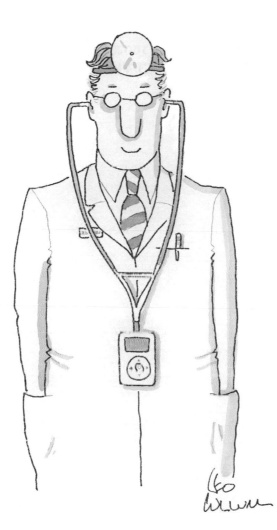

"*Your red and white blood cells are normal. I'm worried about your rosé cells.*"

"Of course I remember you, Dolores. That's the trouble with partial amnesia."

"First I started buying in bulk, then I started eating in bulk."

"The voices have been in my head for years and yet they refuse to learn English."

"You have a generic illness. Generic drugs should work fine."

"I'd be in favor of a 'pay as you go' healthcare system."

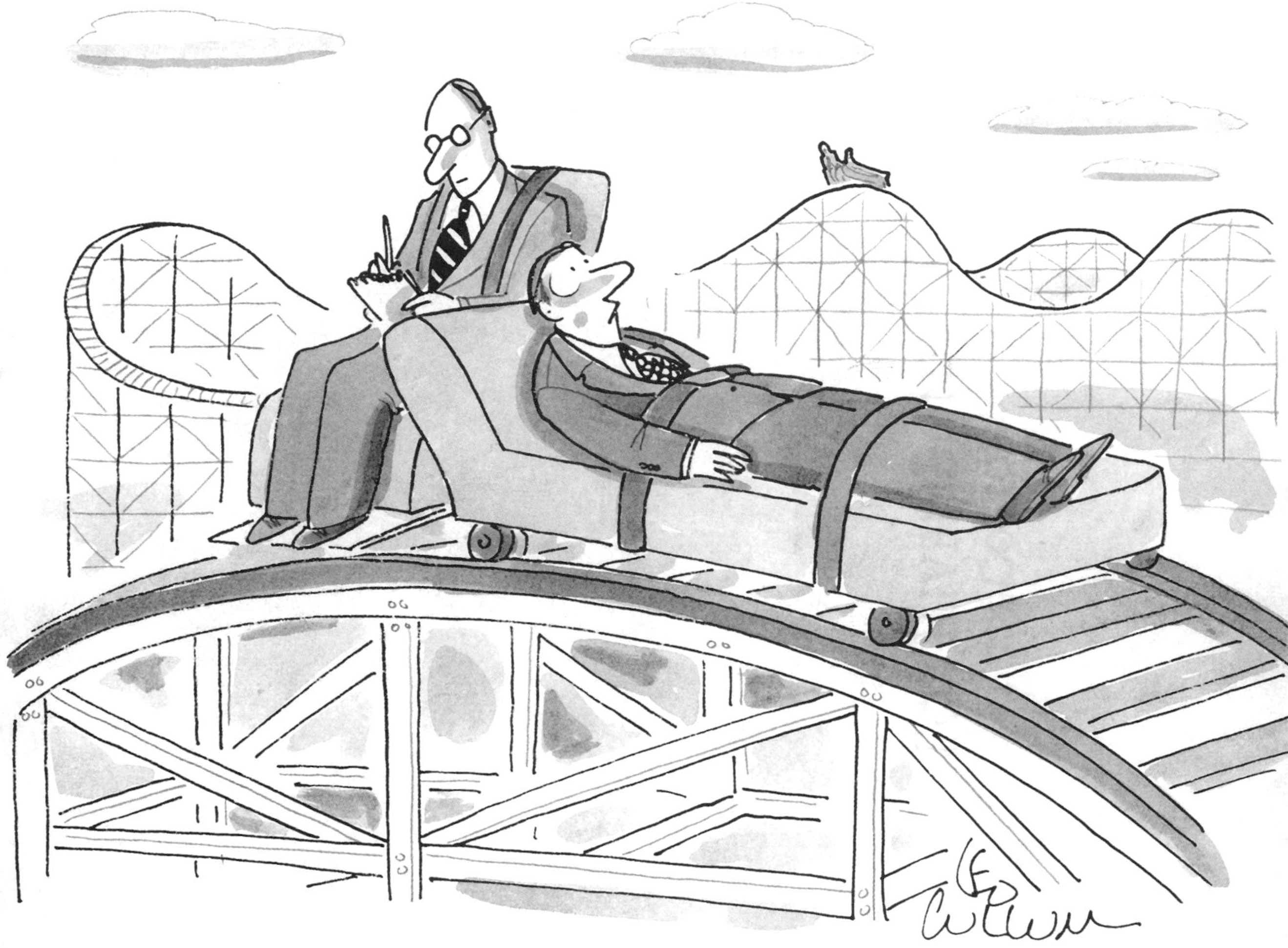

"*That one, unfortunately, is my blood pressure.*"

"All I remember is a big explosion in the lab and the next thing I knew I was living in Scarsdale."

"We could run some tests but I'm certain they're just goose bumps."

"You're lucky. This is a great city to be sick in."

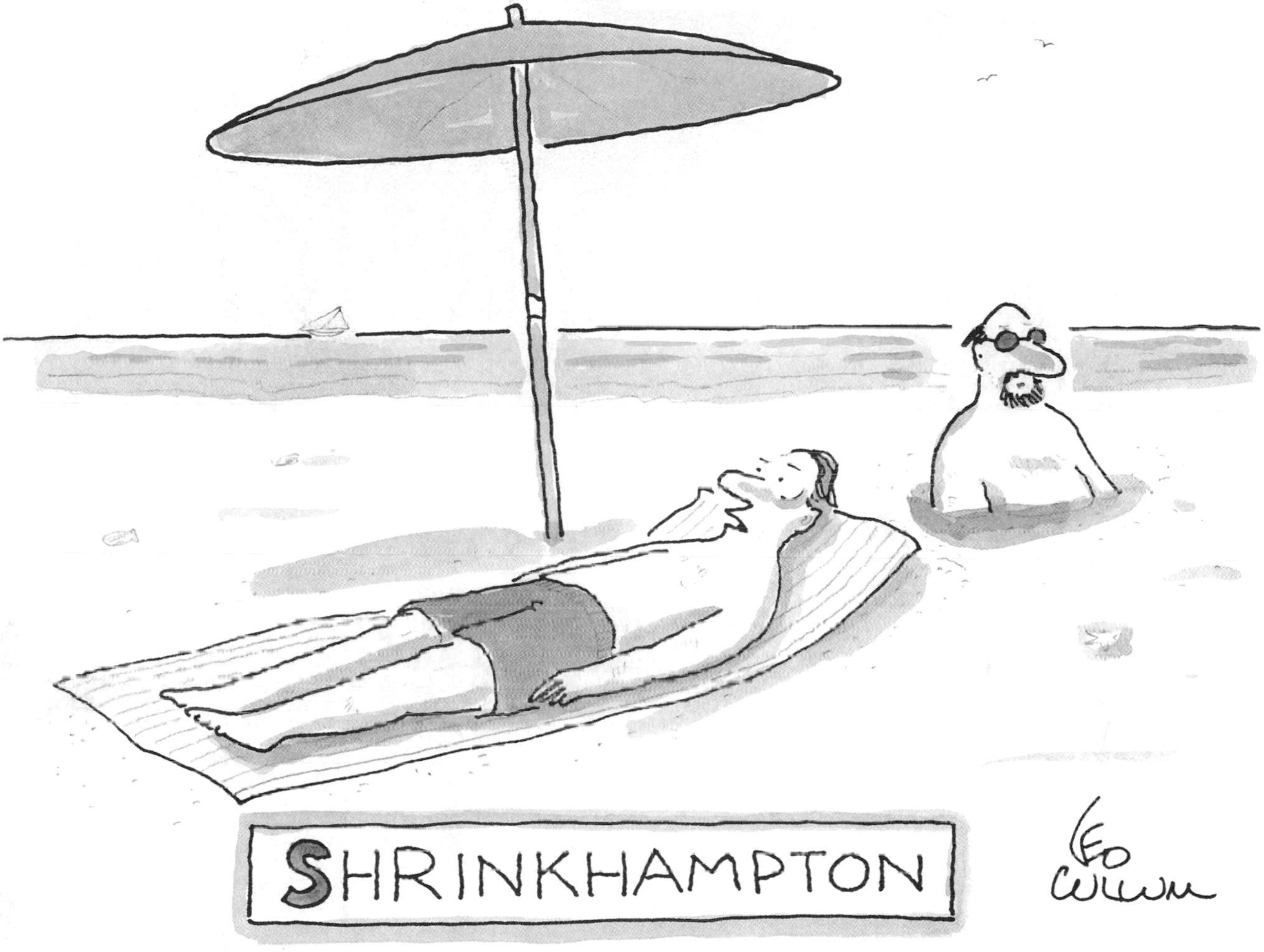
SHRINKHAMPTON
LEO CULLUM

"The surgery of course is elective and I vote yes!"

"It could be postpartum depression. I'm seeing that in a lot of investors."

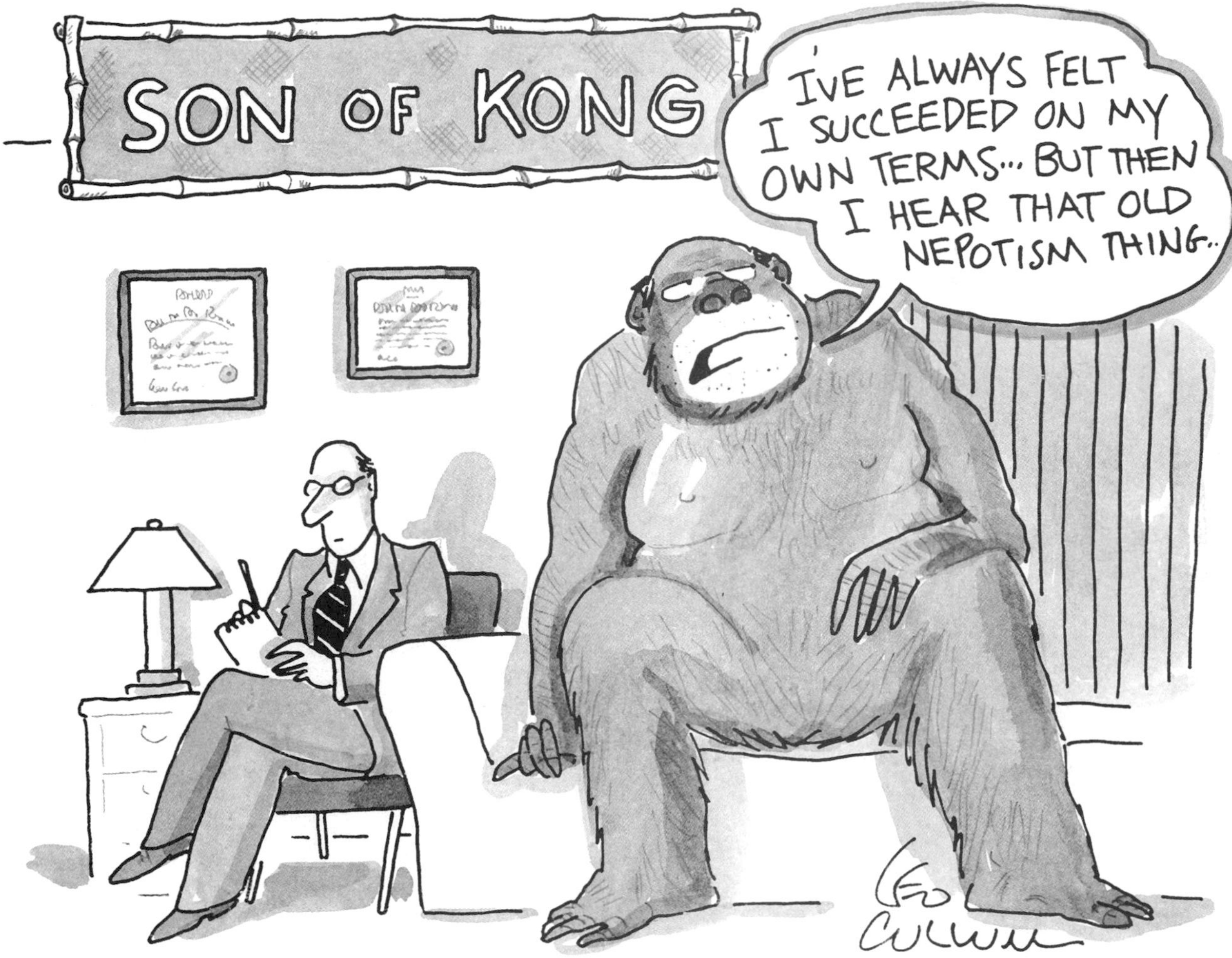
SON OF KONG
I'VE ALWAYS FELT I SUCCEEDED ON MY OWN TERMS... BUT THEN I HEAR THAT OLD NEPOTISM THING..
LEO CULLUM

"I've decided to take up smoking but I'm just starting with the patch."

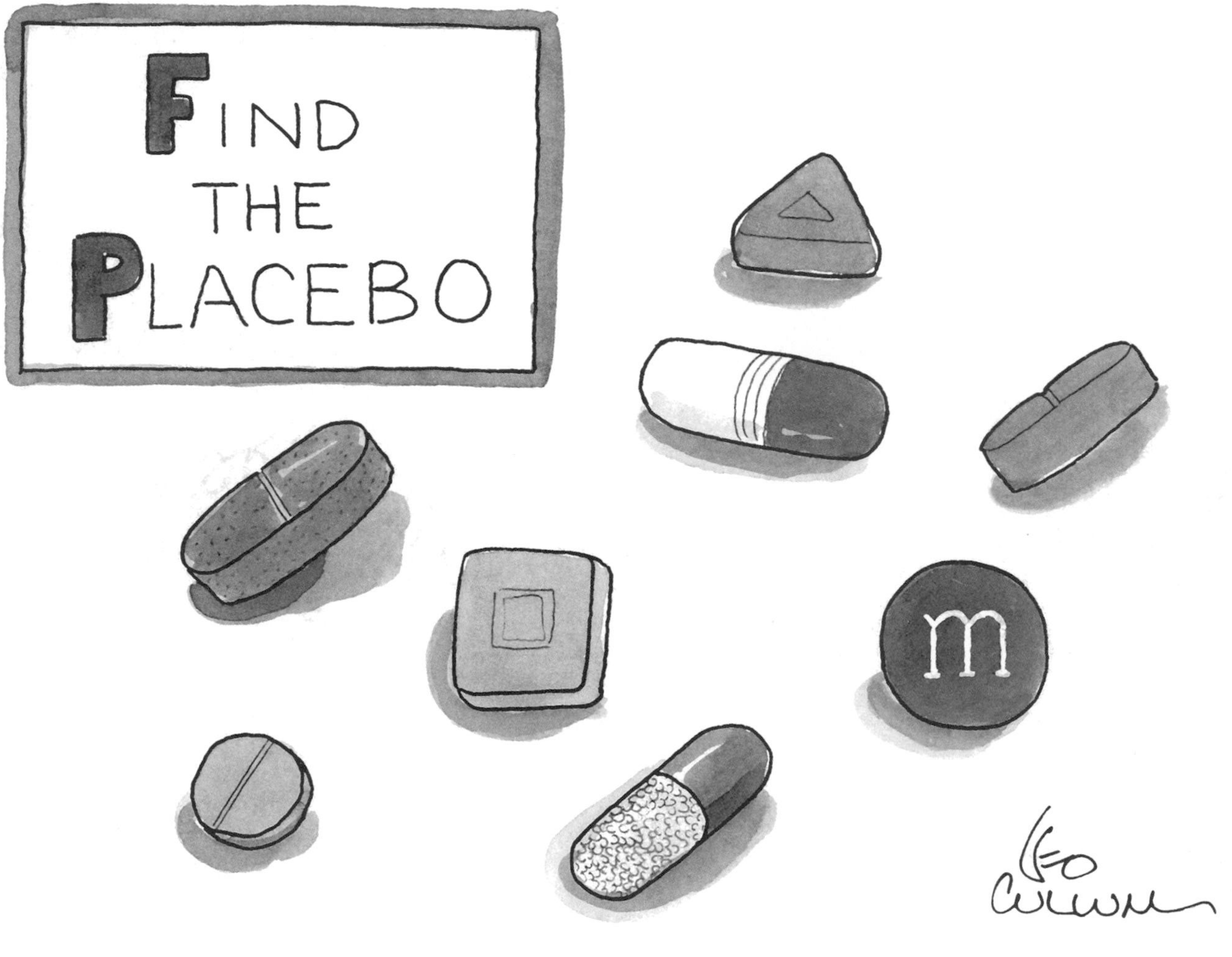
FIND
THE
PLACEBO
m
LEO CULLUM

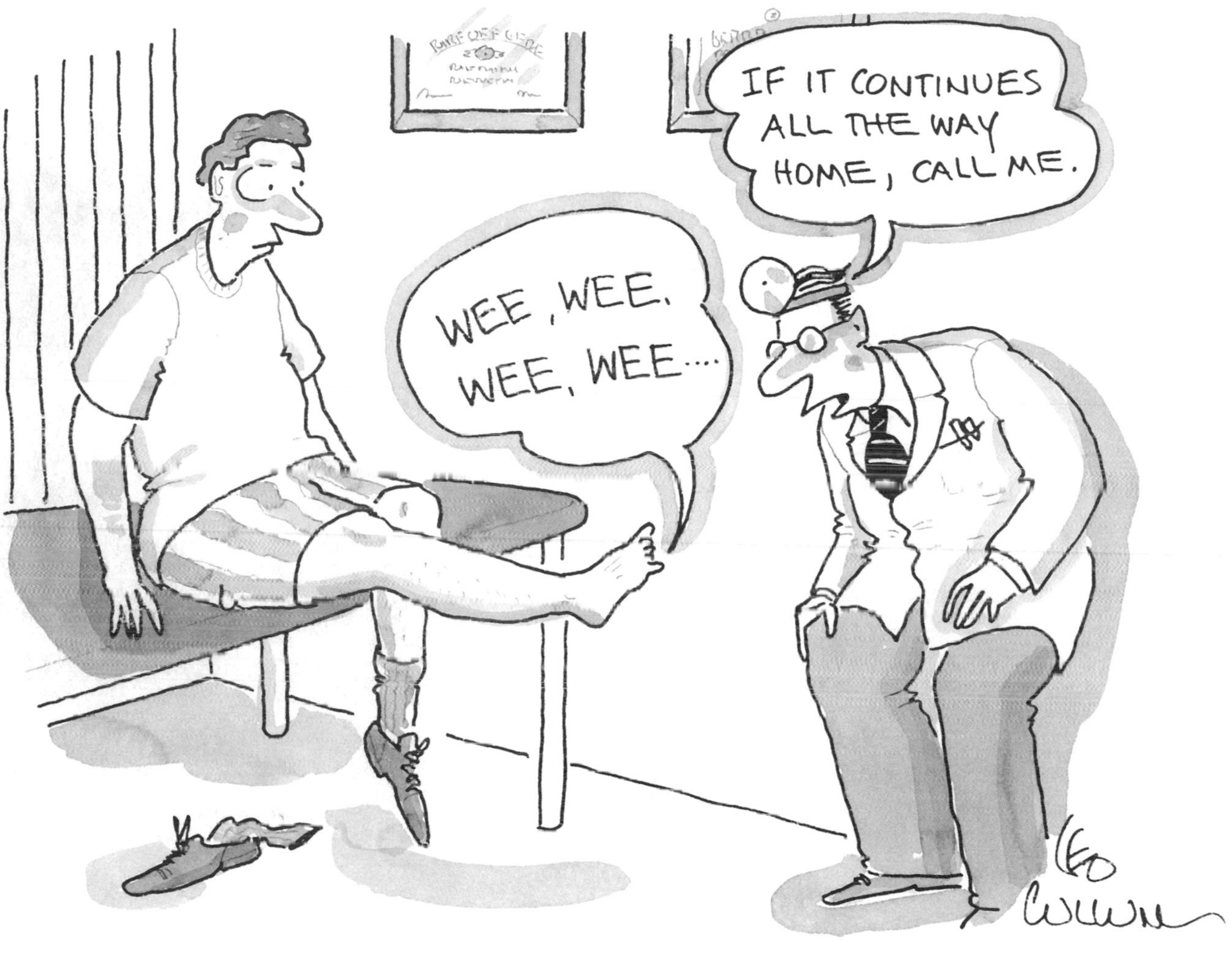
WEE, WEE,
WEE, WEE....
IF IT CONTINUES
ALL THE WAY
HOME, CALL ME.

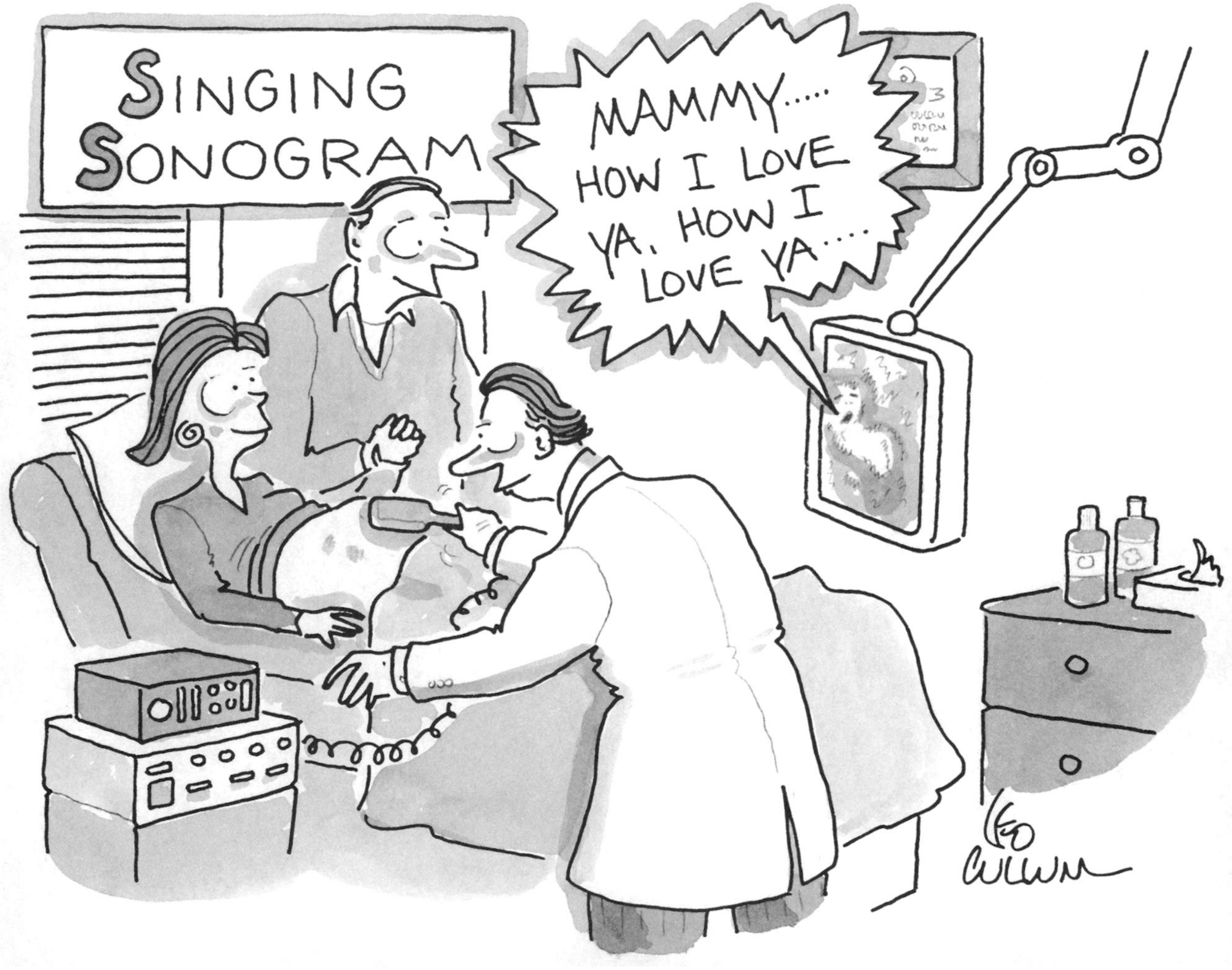
SINGING SONOGRAM
MAMMY..... HOW I LOVE YA, HOW I LOVE YA.....

"*When your skull was open for the surgery, I sprinkled in some potpourri.*"

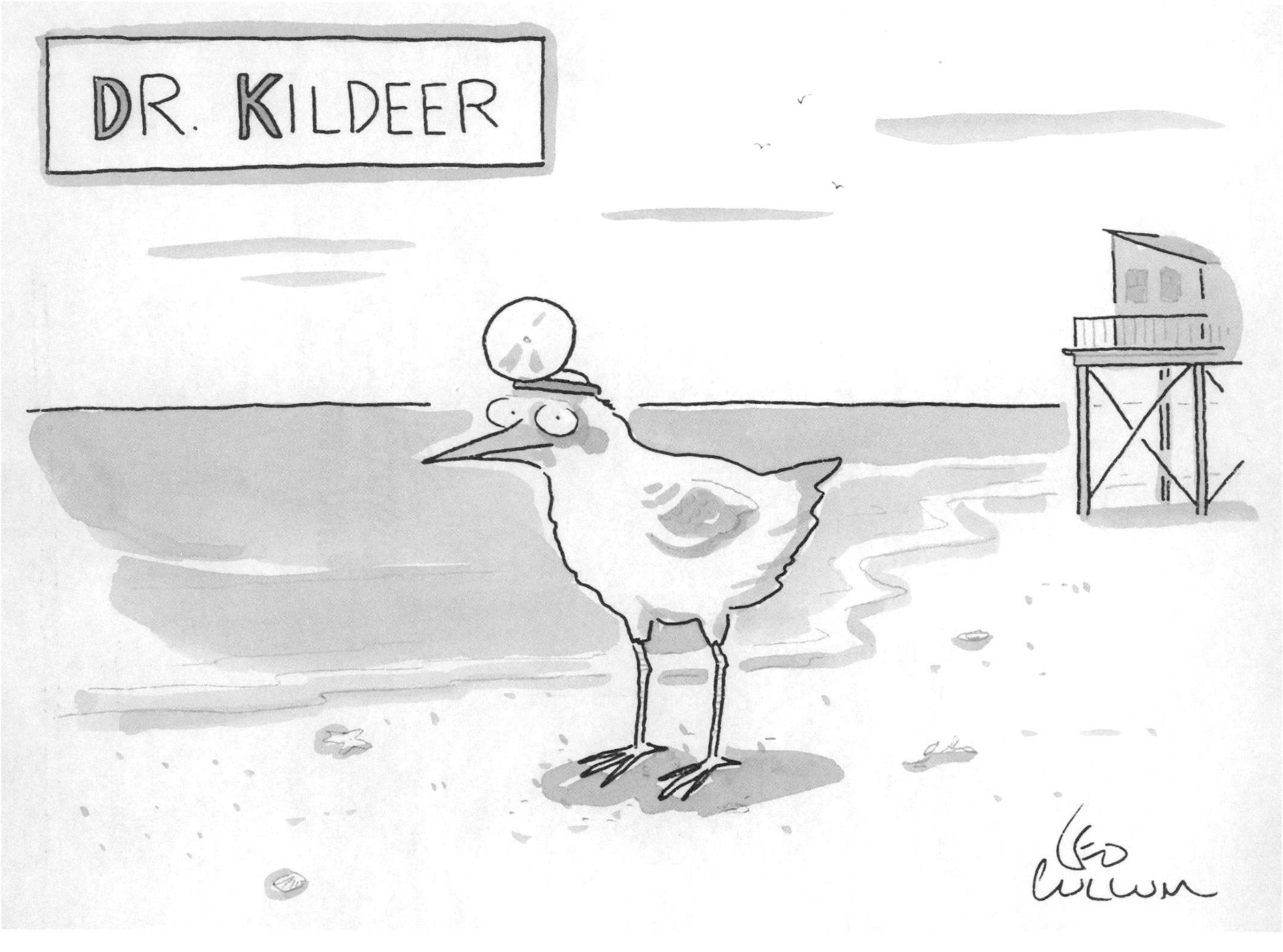
DR. KILDEER
LEO CULLUM

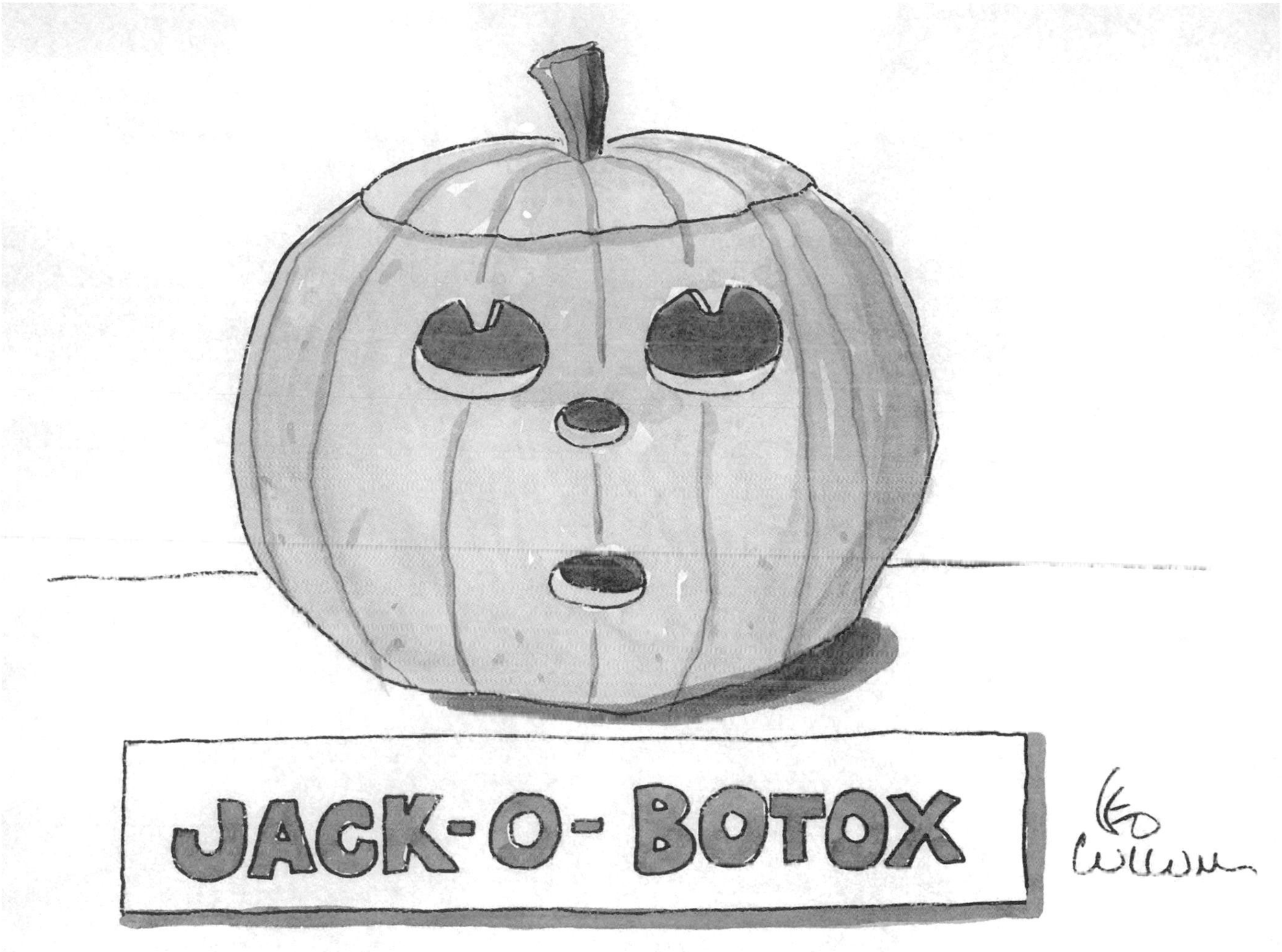
JACK-O-BOTOX

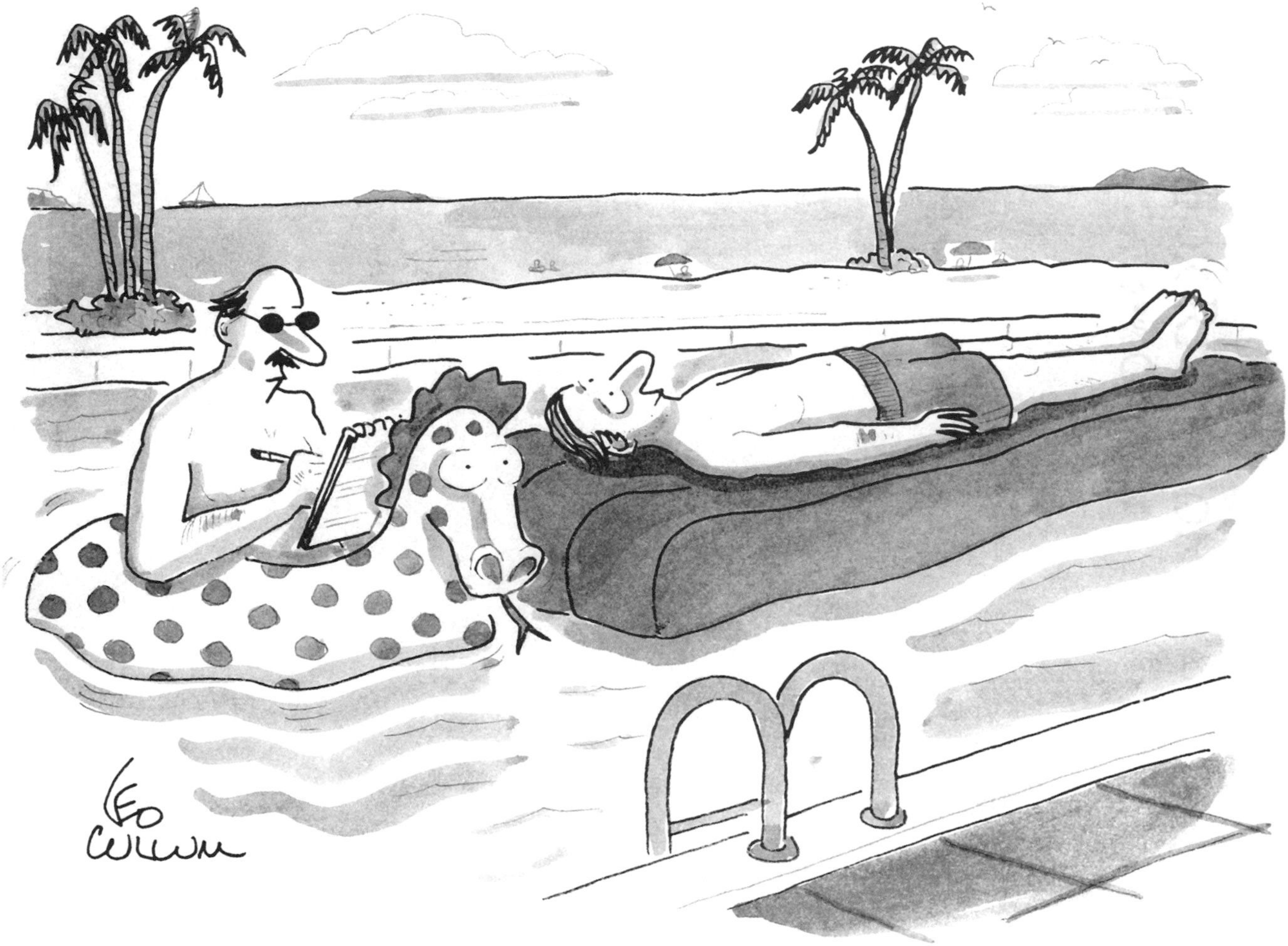

"A vodka martini with two olives? That's just what the doctor ordered."

FOOD
SLEEP
CALIFORNIA
WORK
HEALTH
SEX
ART

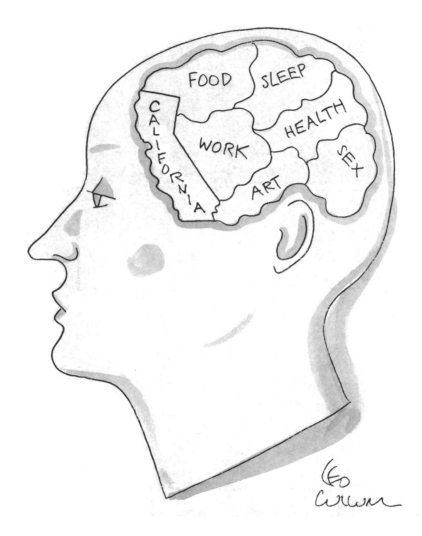

"We've sewn him up but now I can't find my iPod."

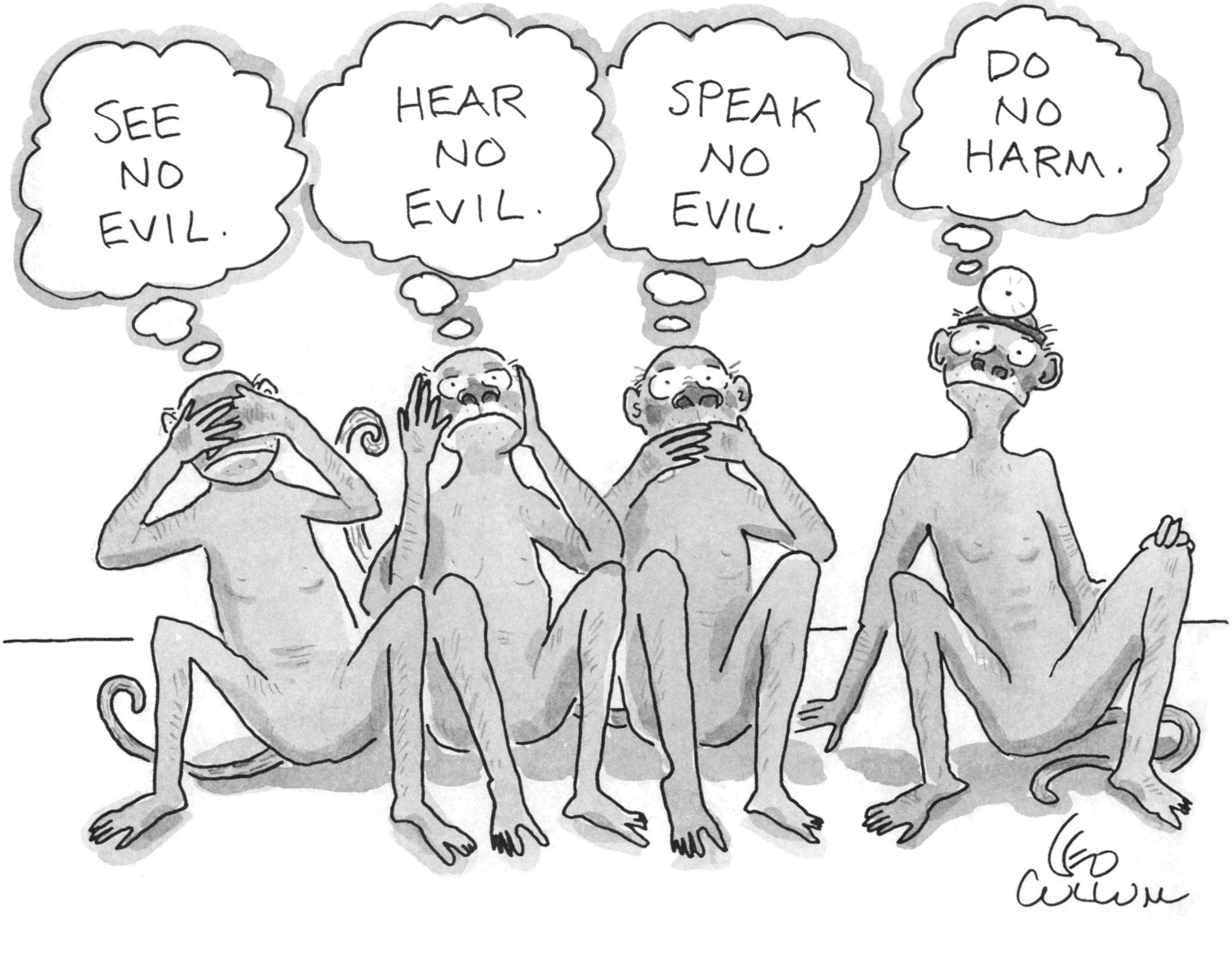
SEE NO EVIL.
HEAR NO EVIL.
SPEAK NO EVIL.
DO NO HARM.

"Read the third line down."

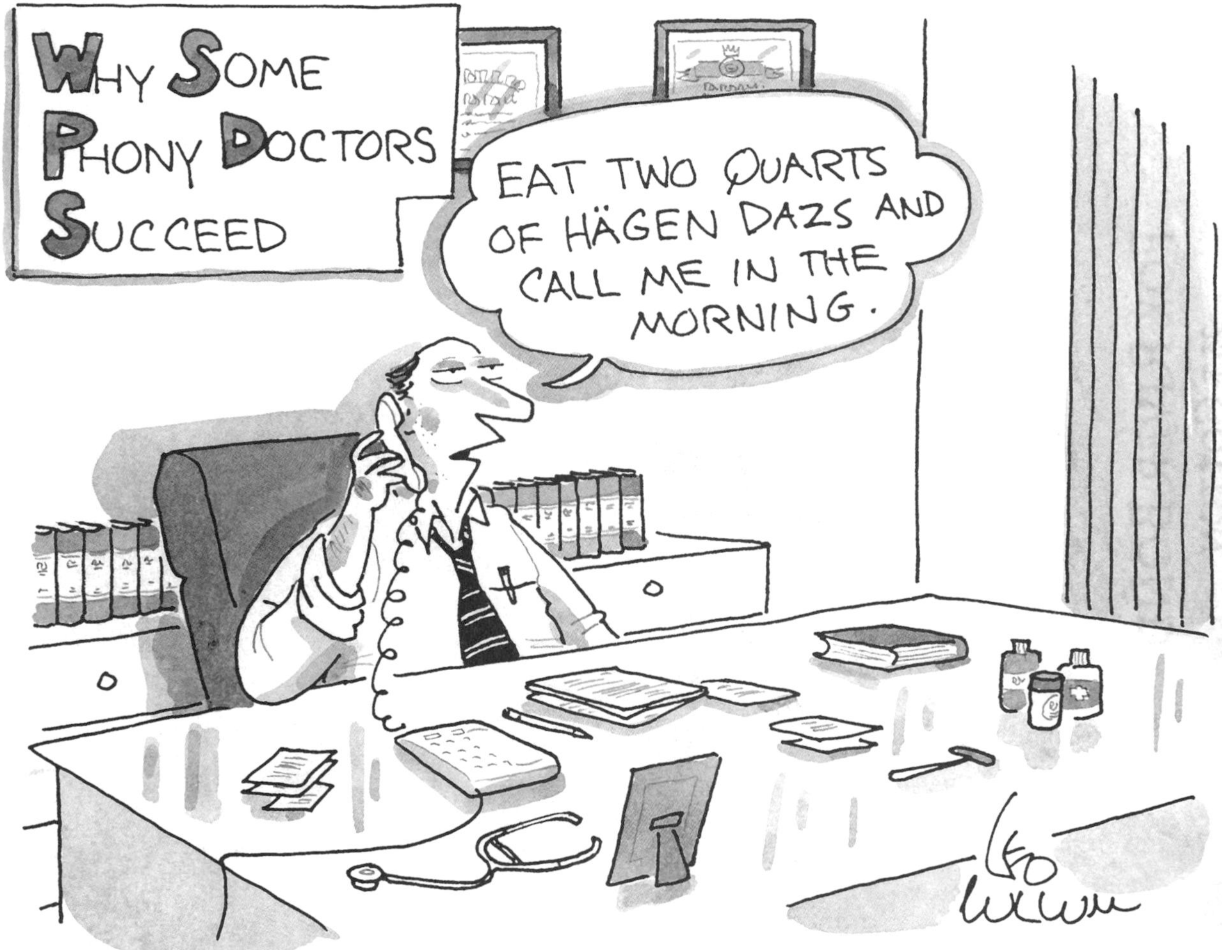
WHY SOME
PHONY DOCTORS
SUCCEED
EAT TWO QUARTS OF HÄGEN DAZS AND CALL ME IN THE MORNING.

"My earliest memory is of Dad saying 'Be proud of your name, Pierce.'"

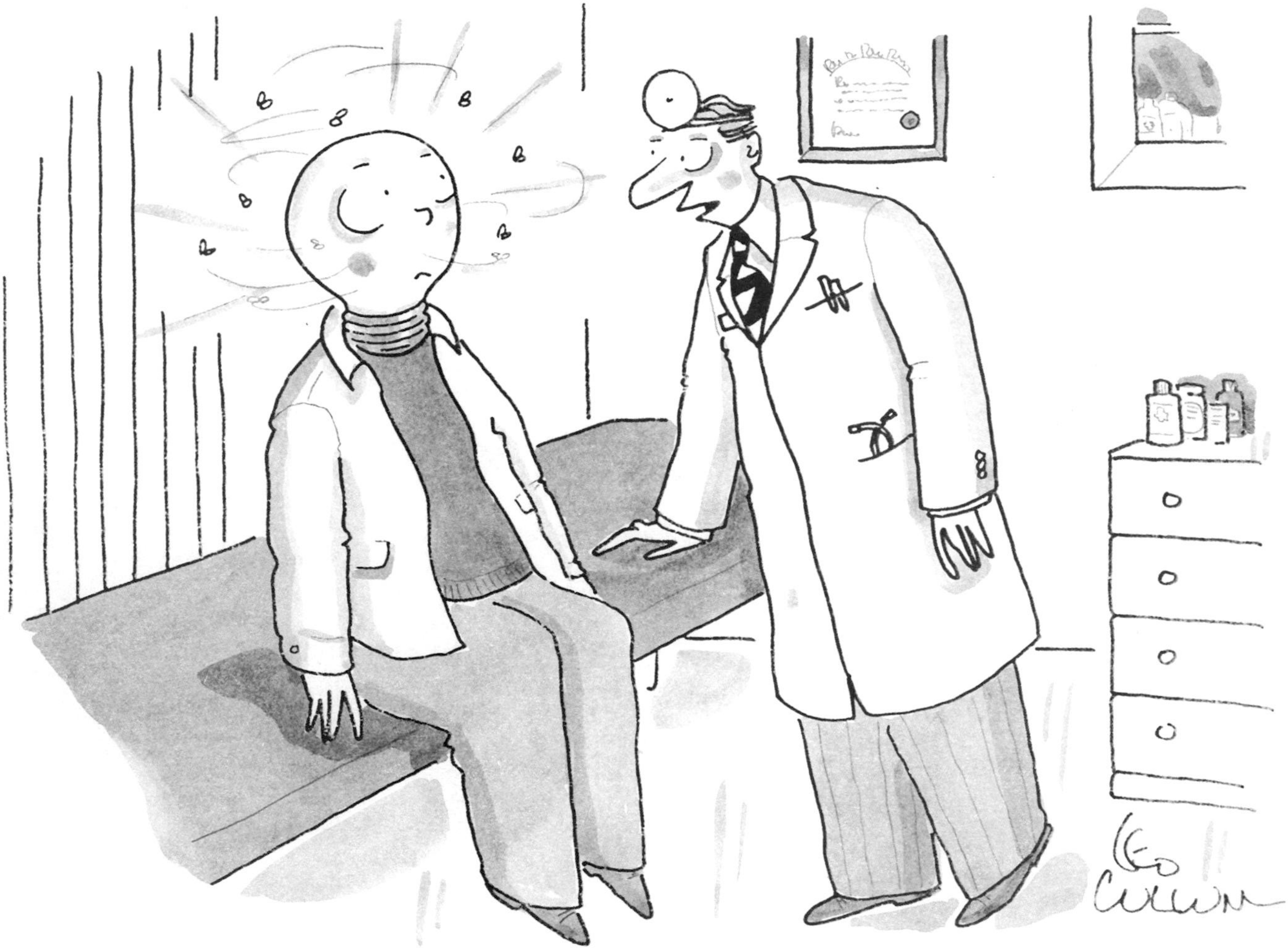

"You've got moths."

"I wish you'd come to me sooner. I'll bet you were a hottie."

"Someone has apparently scooped out your brains and made a pie."

"*You won't actually be seeing the doctor. The doctor is in India.*"

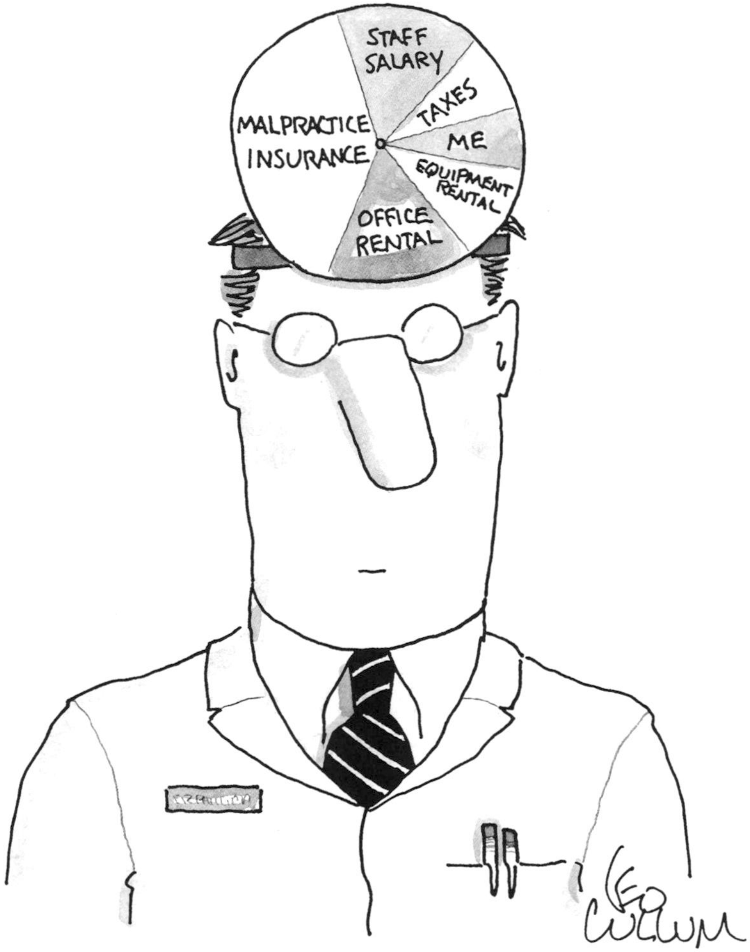
STAFF SALARY
TAXES
ME
EQUIPMENT RENTAL
OFFICE RENTAL
MALPRACTICE INSURANCE

"*You should have this looked at.*"

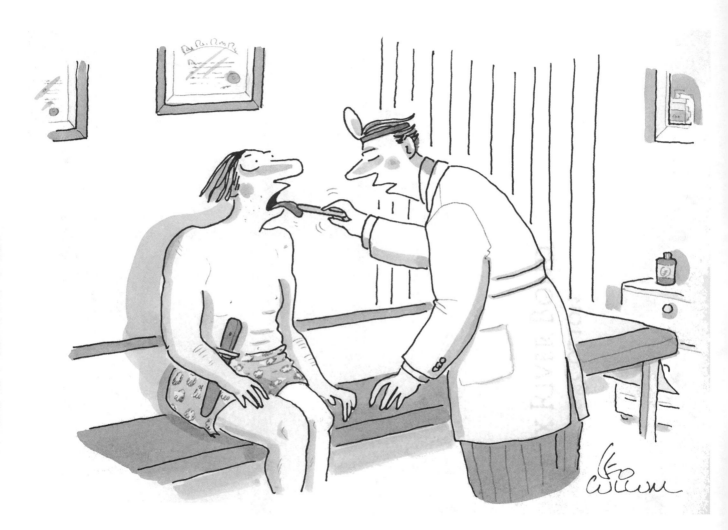

"You've got to stop using the Tarzan yell to impress women."

"Finish it all. Your meds are in there."

"It seems to be effective so we're going to just keep milking you."

"It can't be narcissism. You're much too ugly."

"*I believe I'm secure enough in my own masculinity to undergo a sex change.*"

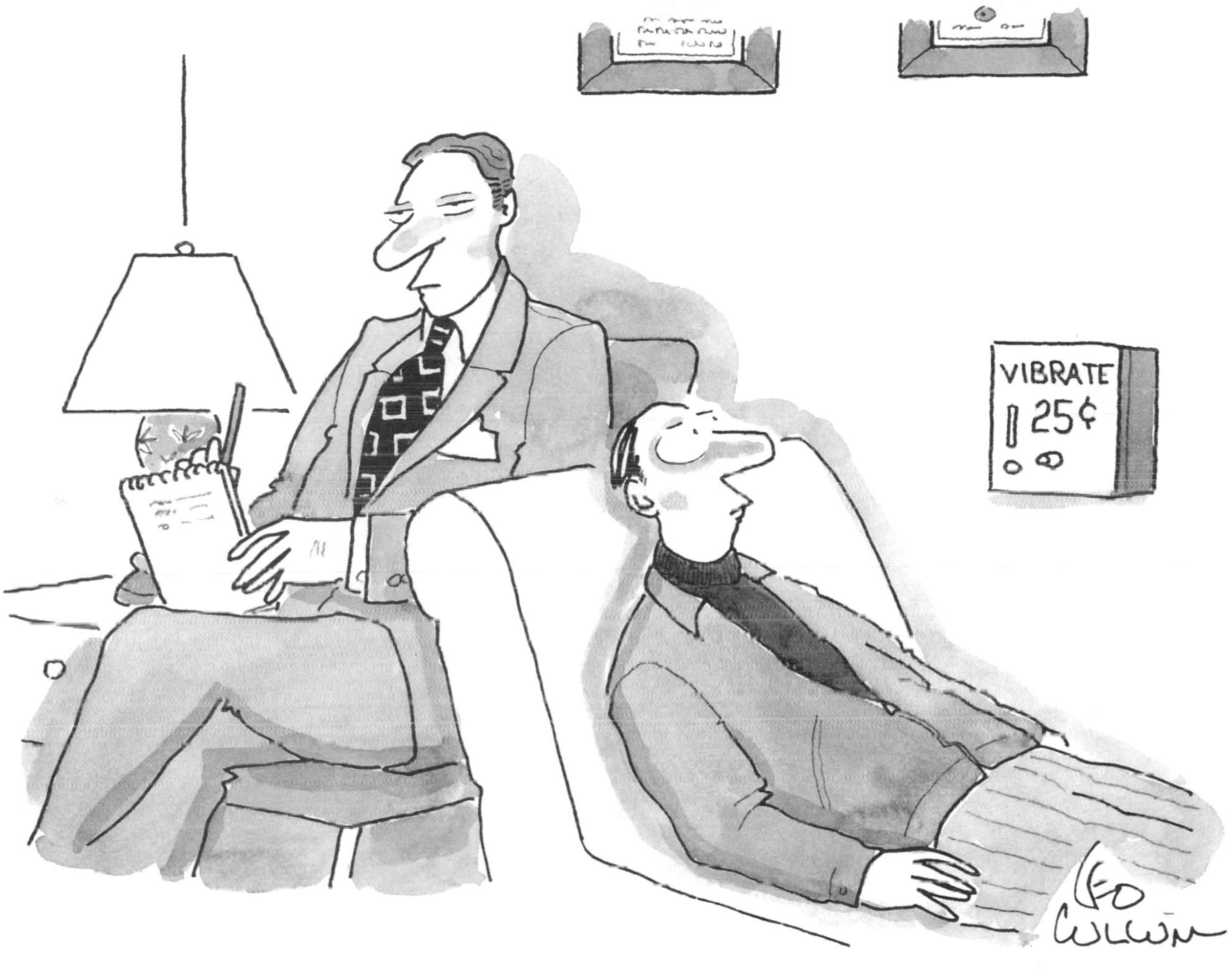
VIBRATE
25¢

"And then, one day, the phone stopped ringing."

"I'll do the Botox but I'll bill it as a thorn in the paw."

"If it's my wife, I'm not all here."

"That's how I hurt my rotator cuff."

"*I never did find out if it was a bird or a plane or Superman.*"

"You mean the zoo doesn't provide coverage?"

"*A second opinion? We can handle that right here.*"

"*You grew up on a farm? I grew up on pharmaceuticals!*"

"It's still in the experimental stage, but I'd like you to try a financial growth hormone."

"*I want it smaller but I still want to look like a rhinoceros.*"

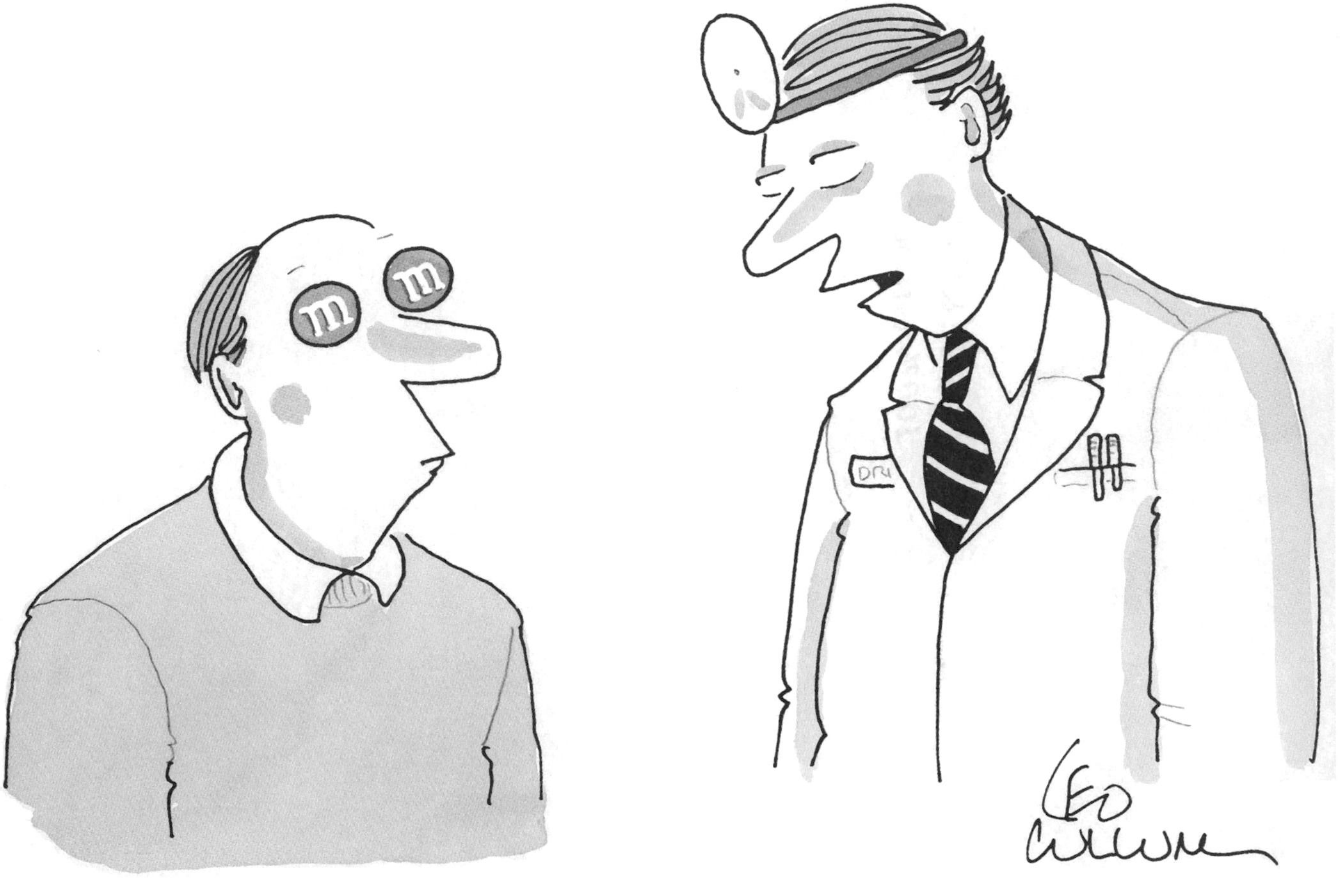
DR
LEO CULLUM

"Lay off the sweets."

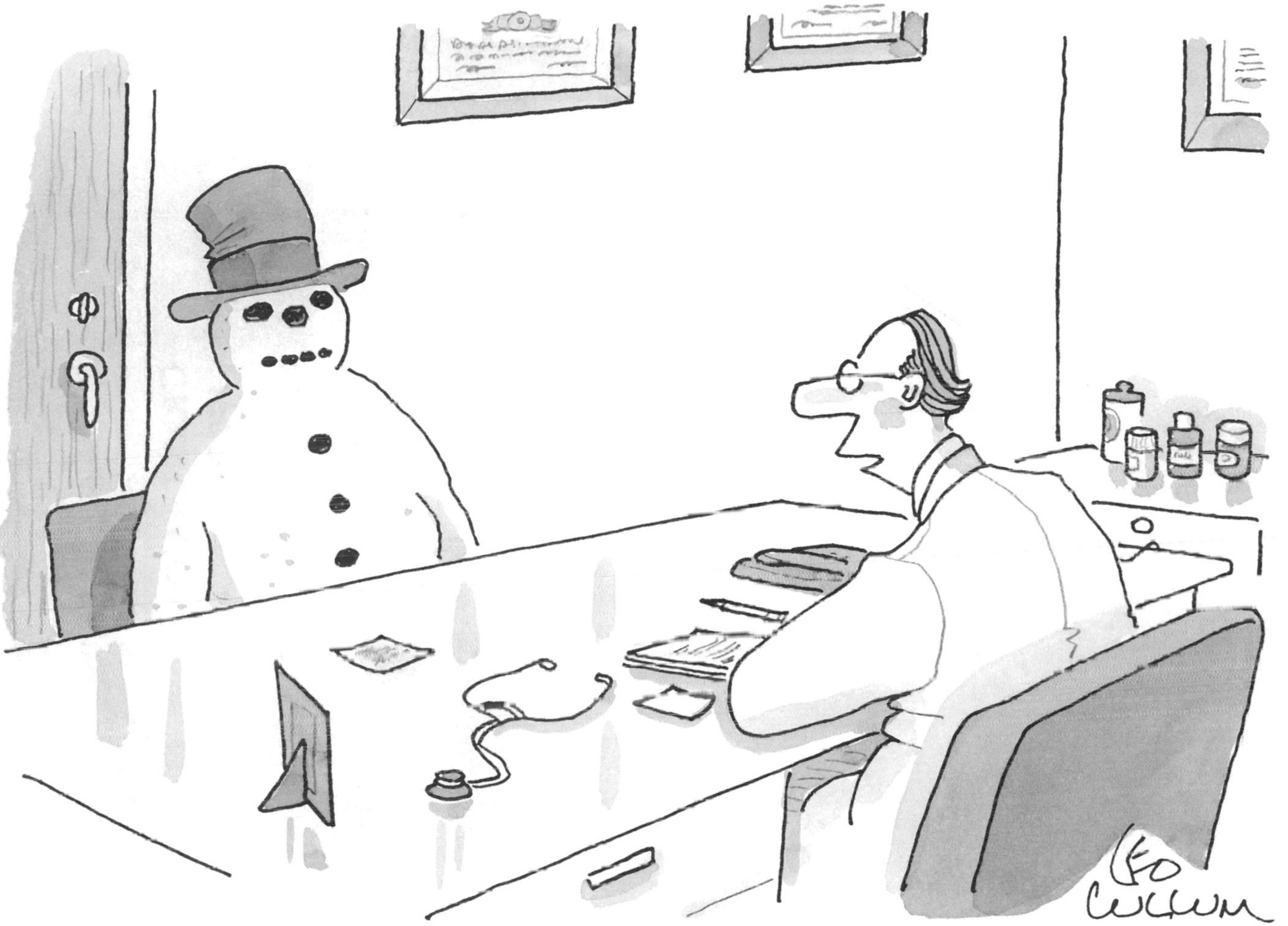

"Stay out of the sun."

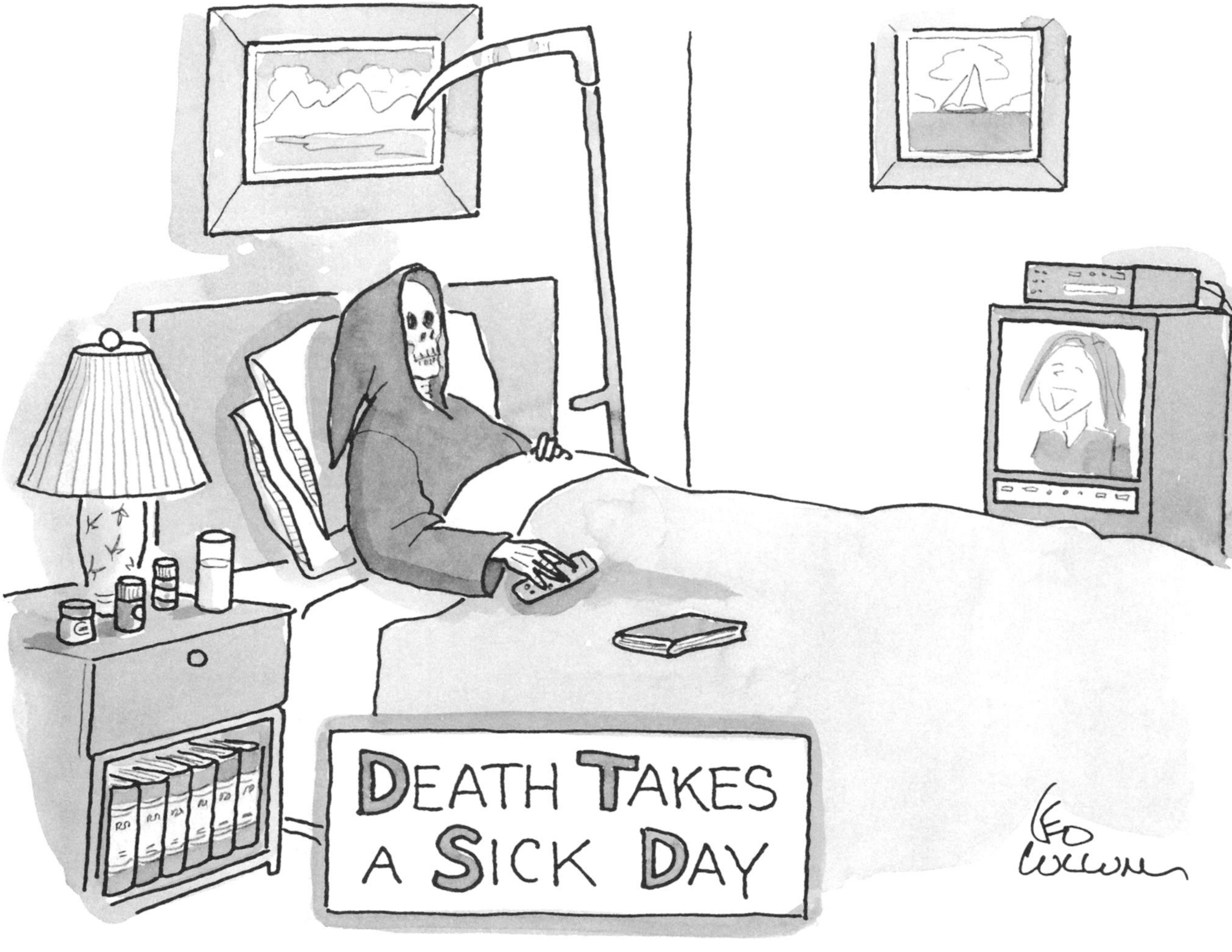
DEATH TAKES
A SICK DAY

"*And just when did your head begin to bobble?*"

"It was a rare, but serious, side effect."

"*I still find myself humming tunes from* Cats."

"I'm having trouble controlling my height."

"I'm not a doctor but I play one in this bar."

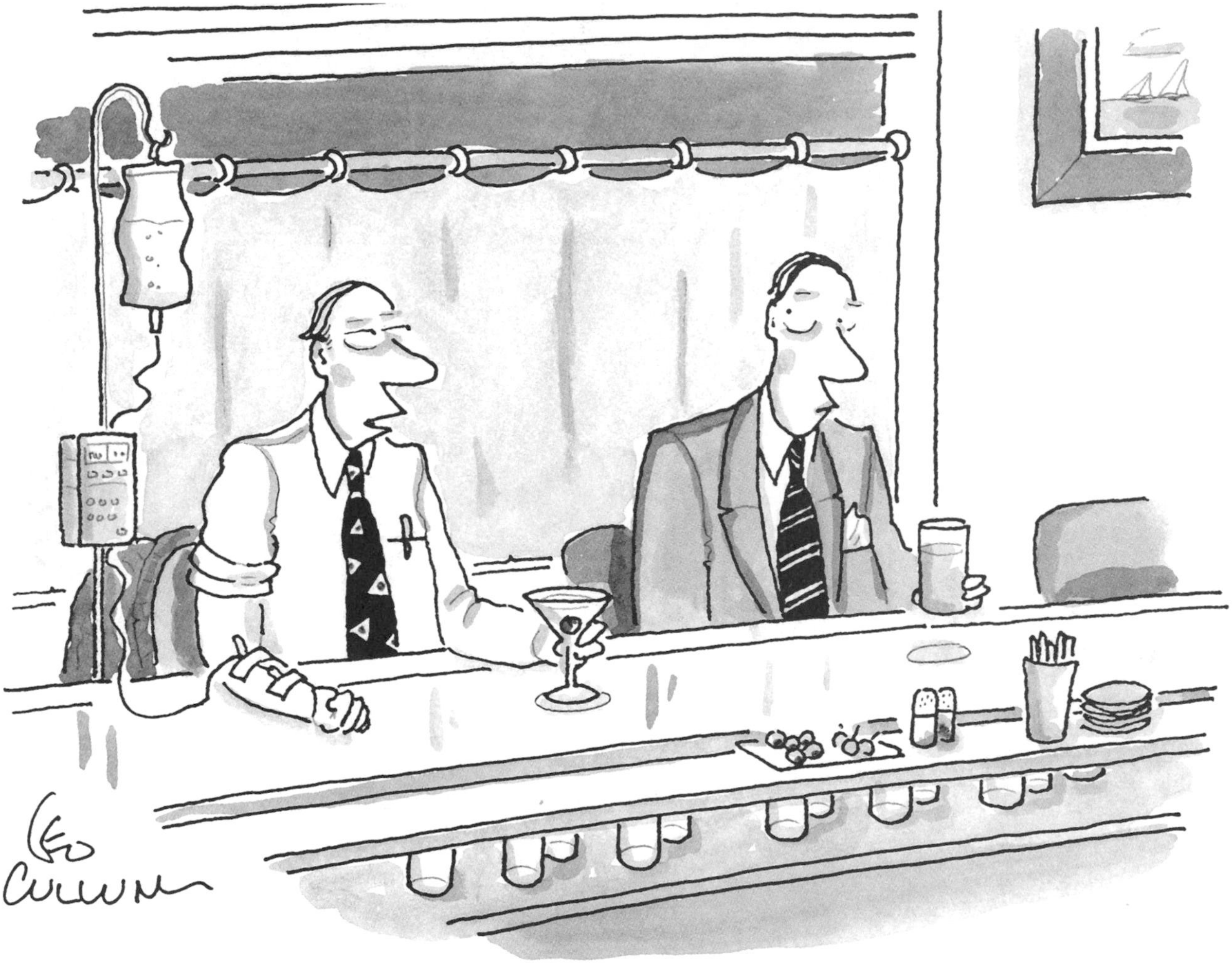
Leo Cullum

"That's the vermouth."

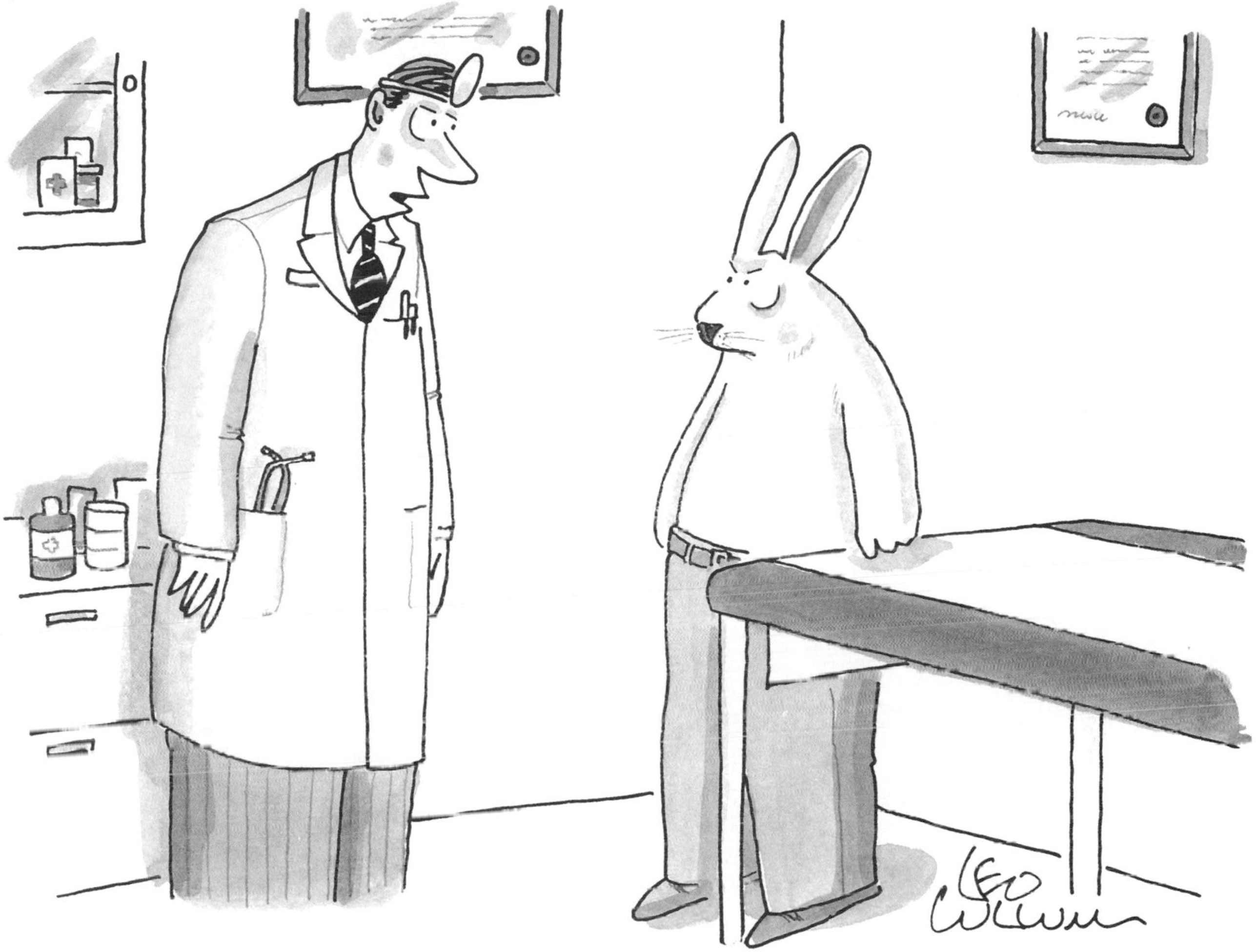

"Hop up on the table."

"In this case the patient was unresponsive, so we turned it over to a collection agency."

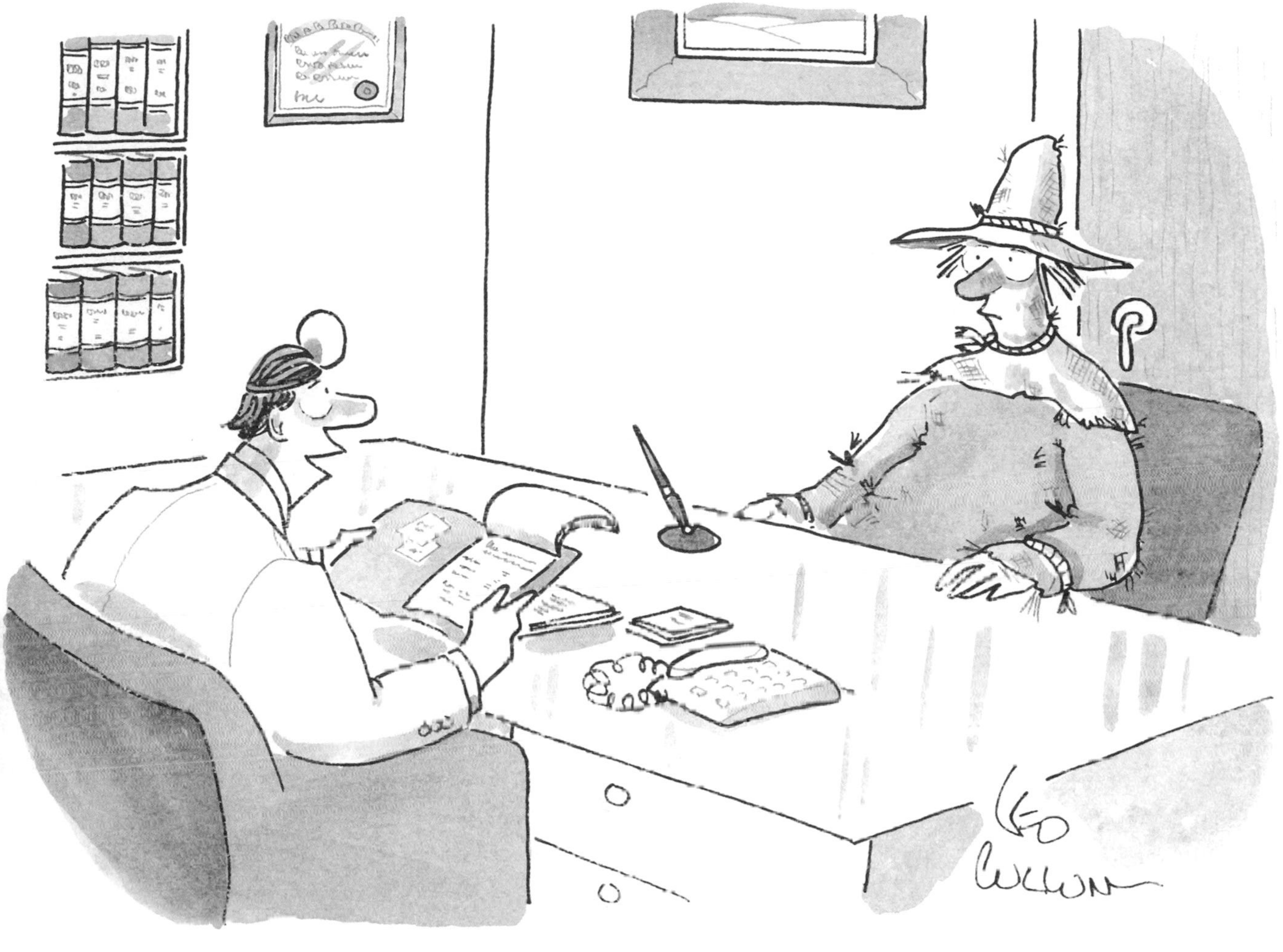

"We can do a brain transplant but you seem to have become a big celebrity without one."

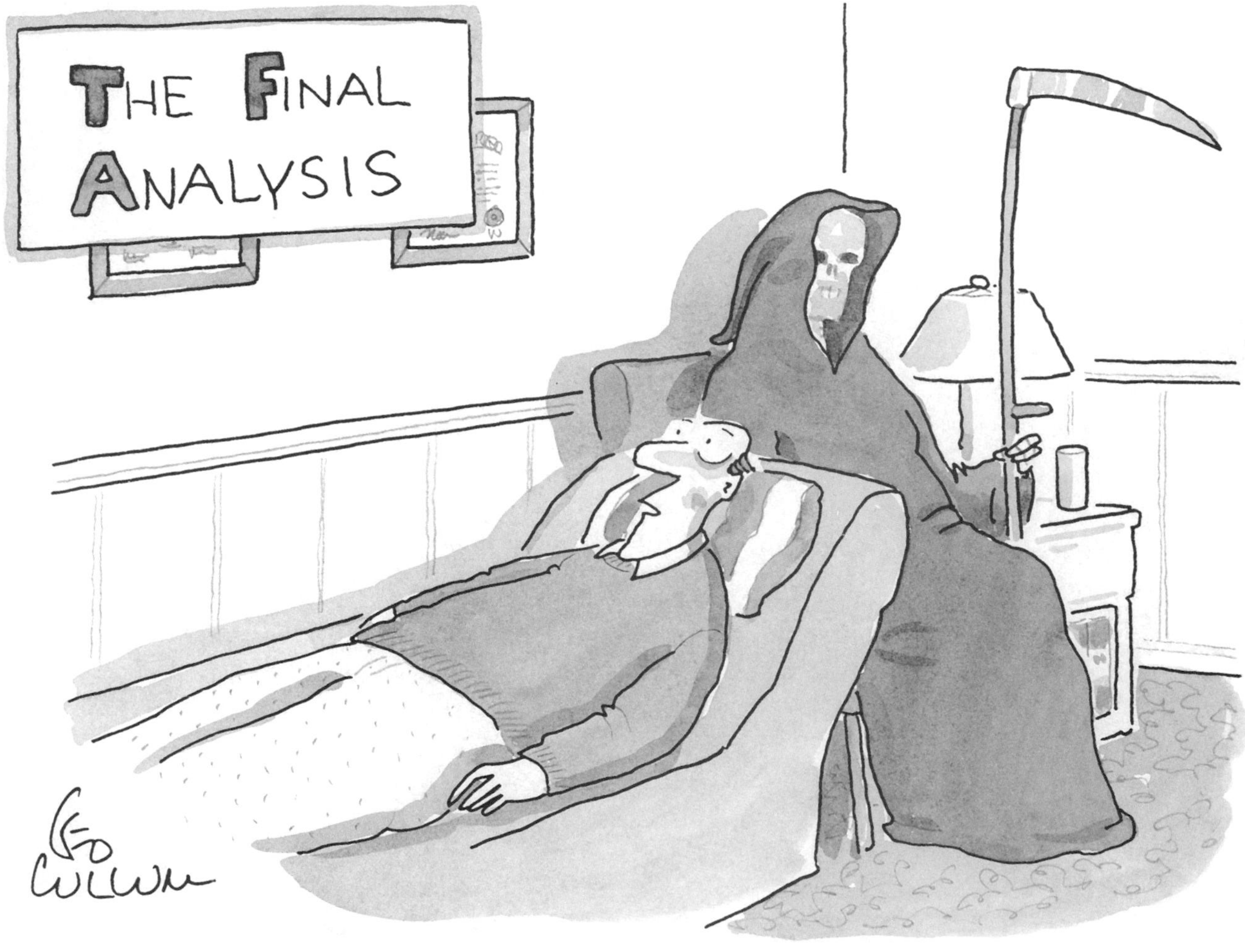
THE FINAL ANALYSIS

"Monkey see? Good! Monkey pay bill!"

"Are you ready for your stress test?"

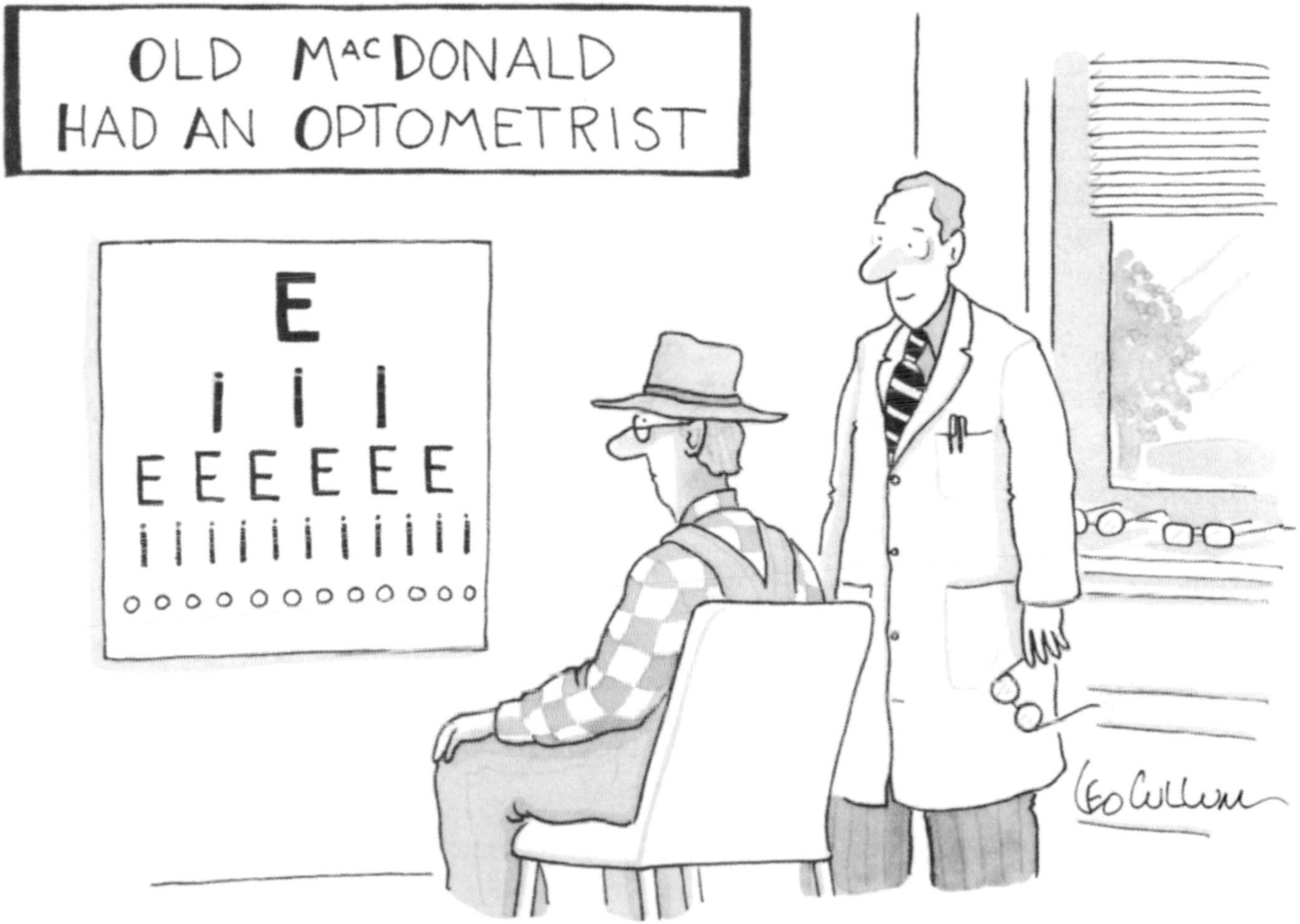
OLD MacDONALD
HAD AN OPTOMETRIST
E
i i i
E E E E E E
i i i i i i i i i i i
o o o o o o o o o o o
LEO CULLUM

"*Well, your nose feels cold.*"

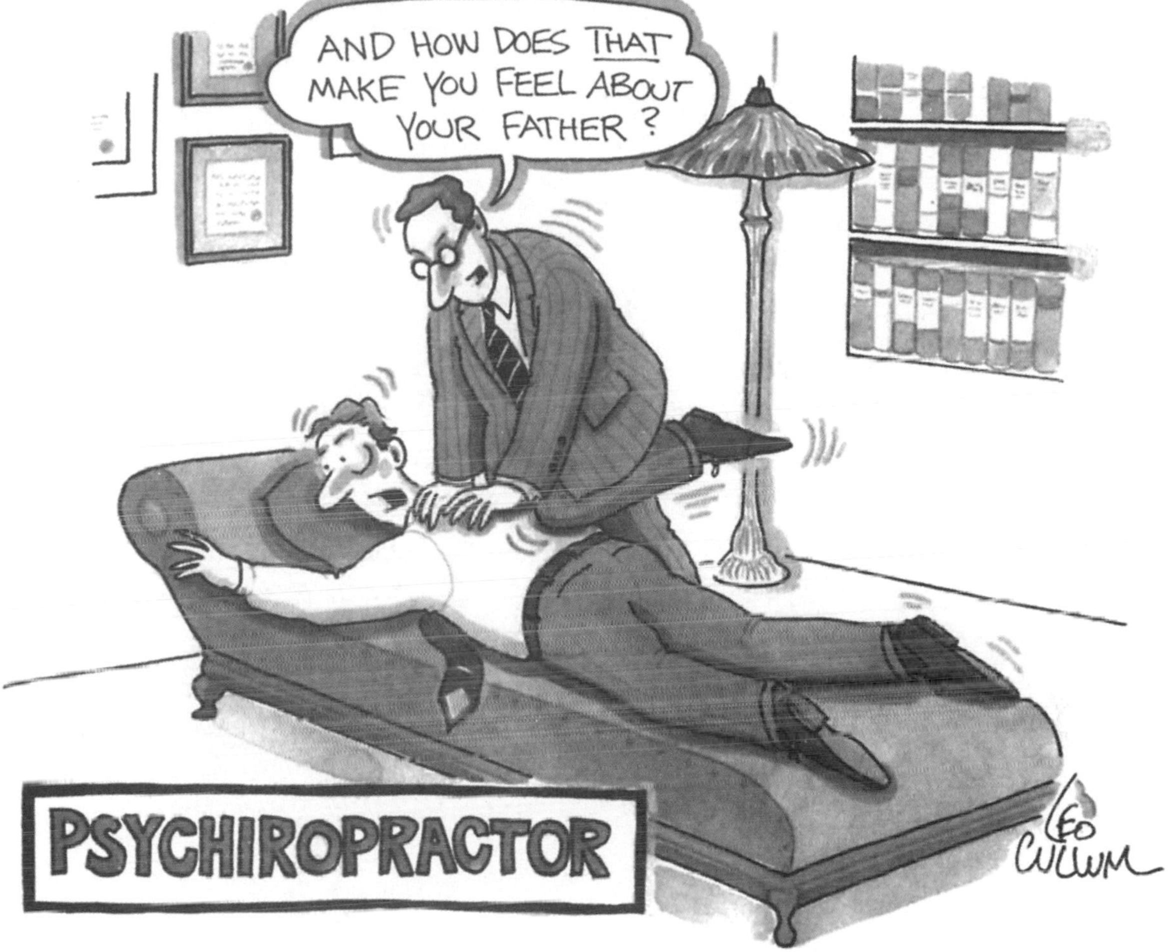
AND HOW DOES THAT MAKE YOU FEEL ABOUT YOUR FATHER?
PSYCHIROPRACTOR
LEO CULLUM

"You need a transplant, but there are very few good parts for middle-aged women."

"When we implant your pacemaker, we can, for a modest additional fee, also implant your cell phone."

"*The ringing in your ears—I think I can help.*"

"*The voices in my head want to sing on* American Idol.*"

"I'd like to help you, but you're in a different HMO."

"*This* is *a second opinion. At first, I thought you had something else.*"

"*Have you popped all those pills I prescribed?*"

"In my practice, I prefer to treat the whole hog."

"*You only* think *you're barking at nothing. We're* all *barking at* something."

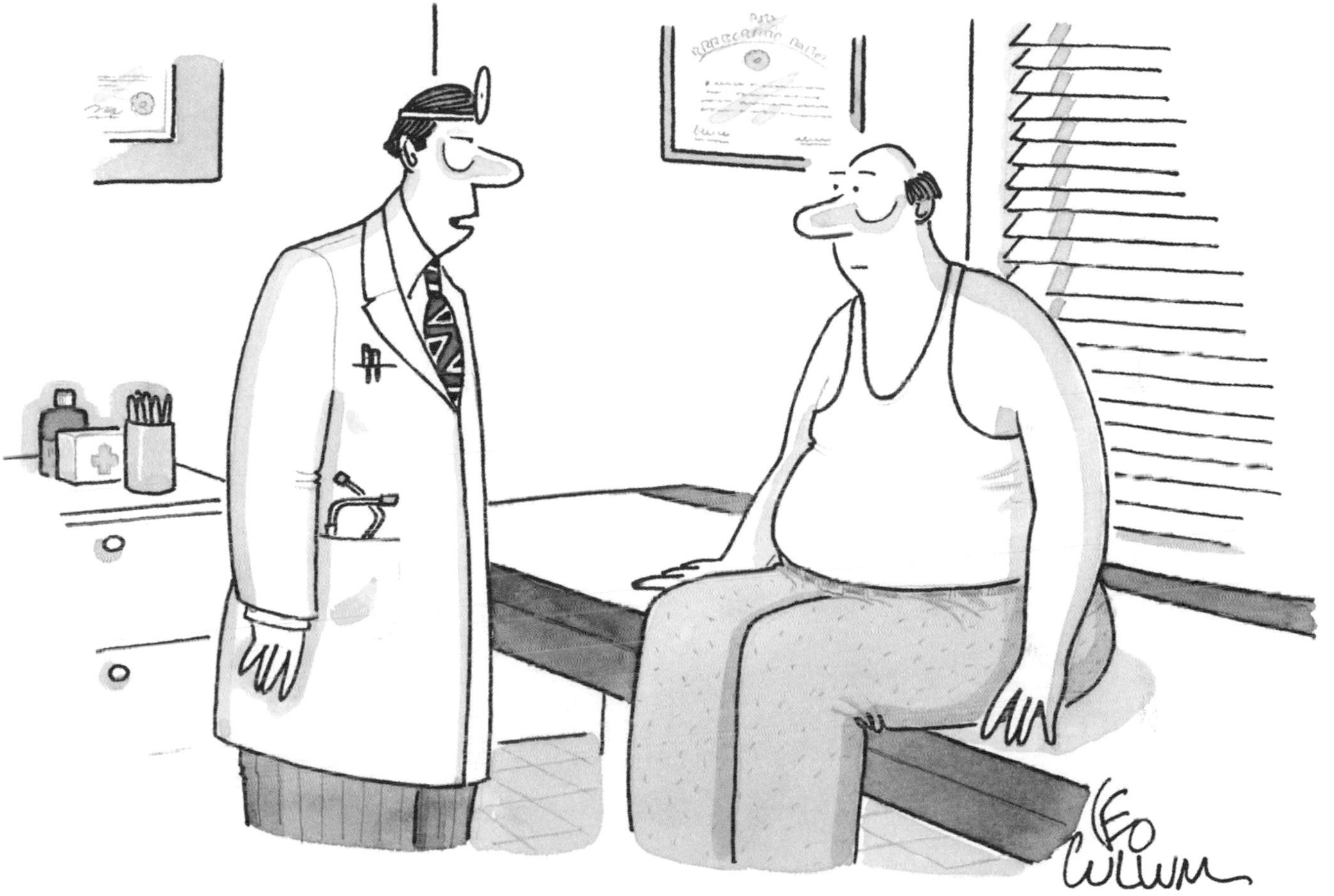

"Your skin is enlarged."

"We could reshape your nose with conventional surgery,
but I'm going to suggest something radical."

"You have a serious illness of an undisclosed nature."

"It is thornlike in appearance, but I need to order a battery of tests."

"*I'm going to be late, dear. It's total craziness here.*"

"I'm not a miracle worker. I can't do the surgery for less than four thousand."

"It could be one of those things that crawls into your ear and lays eggs, and the eggs hatch and burrow into your—nope. It looks fine."

"*Would it be possible to speak with the personality that pays the bills?*"

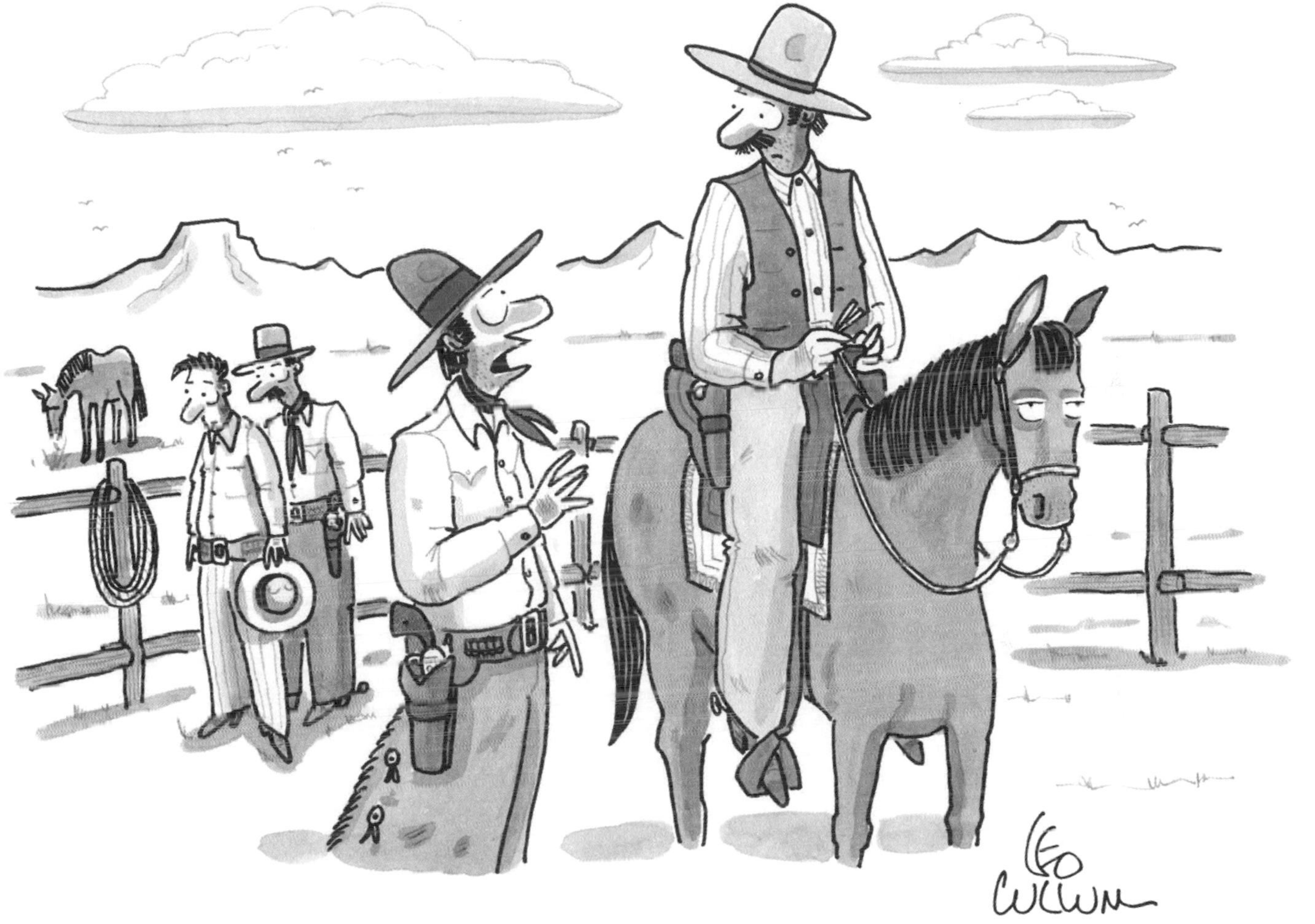

"Slim has a dry scaly patch on his neck! Ride to town and bring the dermatologist."

"*There are many questions, of course, that won't be answered till the autopsy.*"

"It's a good thing you're here. I just punctured your eardrum."

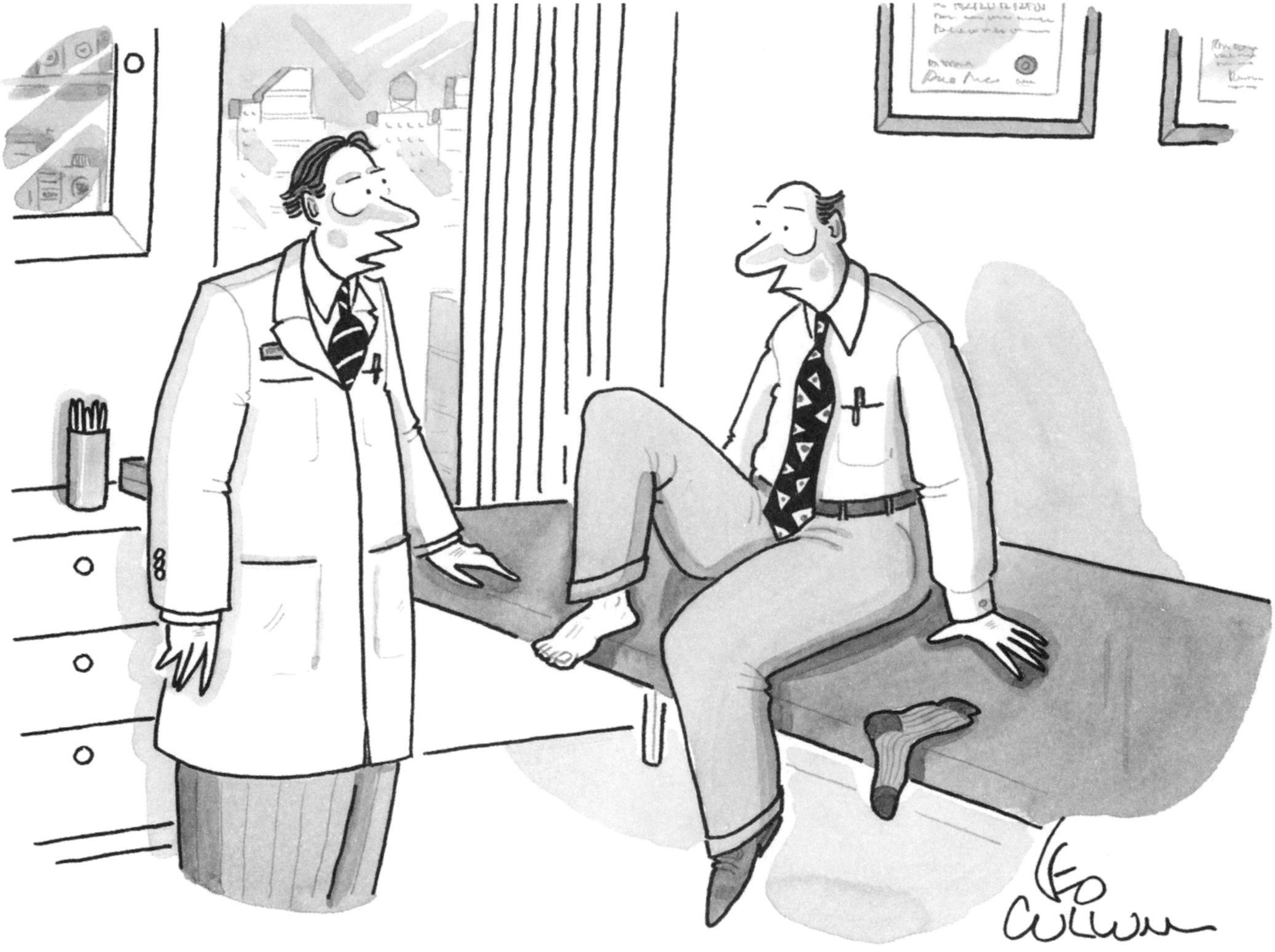

"I'm sorry—I'm a left-foot podiatrist."

"You may believe you've been overcharged, but, remember, you're overmedicated."

"I could prescribe a massive amount of painkillers, but I'm the computer repairman."

"Many women are more at ease with a female doctor. That's why I'm wearing the wig."

"I've got a weak muscle in my eye, and my doctor says the patch will help."

"*You'll be awake during the entire procedure. The anesthesiologist is on vacation.*"

"You're fifty-seven years old. I'd like to get that down a bit."

"After–psychotherapy mint?"

"It's lotto fever."

"It's that same dream, where I'm drowning in a bowl of noodles."

"*Good news. The test results show it's a metaphor.*"

"*Eventually, I'd like to see you able to put* yourself *back together.*"

"I'm right there in the room, and no one even acknowledges me."

"I'd like to get your arrow count down."

"And you're certain these are accidents?"

"Even though you gave the CEO a kidney, this is a lot of sick days."

"Scratch my head, would you?"

"I still have room for a second opinion."

"I'm letting my nemesis define me."